General B.C. Joshi Memorial Lectures
on
NATIONAL SECURITY

General B.C. Joshi Memorial Lectures
on
NATIONAL SECURITY

Foreword by

Prof. (Dr.) Bhushan Patwardhan
Vice-Chairman
University Grants Commission
Bahadur Shah Marg, New Delhi

Edited by

Prof. (Dr.) Nitin R. Karmalkar
Prof. (Dr.) Vijay S. Khare
Department of Defence & Strategic Studies
Dr. Babasaheb Ambedkar Bhavan
Savitribai Phule Pune University
Pune-411007(India)

PENTAGON PRESS LLP

General B.C. Joshi Memorial Lectures on NATIONAL SECURITY

Editors: Prof. (Dr.) Nitin Karmalkar and Prof. (Dr.) Vijay Khare

First Published in 2021

ISBN 978-93-90095-23-0

Published by
PENTAGON PRESS LLP
206, Peacock Lane, Shahpur Jat
New Delhi-110049
Phones: 011-64706243, 26491568
Telefax: 011-26490600
email: rajan@pentagonpress.in
website: www.pentagonpress.in

Printed at Aegean Offset Printers, Greater Noida, U.P.

Dedicated to

Brave Soldiers who scarified their lives

for India's Unity, Integrity and Security

Contents

विश्वविद्यालय अनुदान आयोग
University Grants Commission
(मानव संसाधन विकास मंत्रालय, भारत सरकार)
(Ministry of Human Resource Development, Govt. of India)
बहादुरशाह ज़फर मार्ग, नई दिल्ली-110002
Bahadur Shah Zafar Marg, New Delhi-110002
Ph.: 011-23214464 (Office)
Fax: 011- 23237143
E-mail: vcm.ugc@nic.in

ज्ञान-विज्ञान विमुक्तये

डॉ. भूषण पटवर्धन
उपाध्यक्ष

Dr. Bhushan Patwardhan
Vice-Chairman

FOREWORD

We are witnessing current scenario when the words of General Joshi who proclaimed that "the 21st Century will be the India Century" are becoming the reality. At this juncture, on the occasion of 25 years of signing a Memorandum of Understanding with the Indian Army, the Department of Defence and Strategic Studies (DDSS), Savitribai Phule Pune University (SPPU) is publishing a composite volume of the General BC Joshi Memorial Lectures. This prestigious memorial lecture was instituted by SPPU in the memory of Gen B C Joshi who passed away on 18 November 1994. I clearly recall that SPPU had published a book focused on National Security, which contained a General B.C. Joshi Memorial Lectures delivered between 1995 to 2005. This book also included Gen Joshi's address on 'Role of Universities Towards the Armed Forces' delivered on 13 November 1994, just five days before he passed away, it is the vision of both late Gen Joshi and late Professor S C Gupte, the then Vice Chancellor to fructify Army-University partnership in a unique way. One of the University Gates that is connected to the defence establishments is named as Gen B C Joshi Dwar as a mark of University-Army collaboration. The institution of Chhatrapati Shivaji Chair on Policy Studies that hosts the Indian Army Resident Scholars Programme is another example of Army-Academia linkage. The Southern Army Command and the University created a corpus to institute the B C Joshi Memorial Lecture whose first lecture in 1995 was delivered by Shri Nani Palkhivala. Since then, the Gen B C Joshi Memorial Lecture on National Security is delivered every year in rotation only by one of the three serving Service Chiefs.

I consider it a privilege to write the Foreword to this valuable book. I have been associated with the University and witness to DDSS-Indian Army ongoing partnership developing over the past three decades. The composite volume of B C Joshi Memorial Lecture consisting of 17 lectures starting from 2004 to 2019 has been jointly edited by Professor Nitin Karmalkar, Vice Chancellor SPPU and Professor Vijay Khare Head DDSS. I would like to take this opportunity to record the contribution of Professor

Gautam Sen, Sawarkar Chair Professor and former Head DDSS who also shaped the National Institute of Strategic and Defence Studies (NISDA), which was funded by the University Grants Commission. It is heartening to see the legacy has been furthered by his successors Professor Shrikant Paranjpe and Professor A S Dalvi and presently Professor Vijay Khare who has extended the collaboration between the Indian Air Force and the DDSS. In the changing geopolitical scenario, India is playing a pivotal role as envisaged by Gen B C Joshi. I am sure in years to come these lecture contents articulated by such a galaxy of decorated defence chiefs will be inspirational to further our strategic culture, augment security, safeguard unity, enhance integration and national interest.

Professor Bhushan Patwardhan
Vice Chairman
University Grants Commission
Bahadur Shah Marg
New Delhi

Preface

We are happy that on the occasion of Silver Jubilee of General B.C. Joshi Memorial Lecture series on behalf of the Department of Defense and Strategic Studies Savitribai Phule Pune University has brought out a book comprising the General B.C. Joshi Memorial Lectures that have been delivered at the Savitribai Phule Pune University from 1995 to 2020.

General Joshi was unique in many ways. He had an immense desire to bring about a cultural change in the thinking process within the Army and convinced that the way to bring about such a change was by exposing service personnel to higher education. He operationalized his intents by forging institutional linkages with the Universities in India. He always had had special feelings and an attachment for Savitribai Phule Pune University from the day he became the Southern Army Commander at Pune. He delivered the Convocation Address in the convocation ceremony held at the Savitribai Phule Pune University, and laid the foundation stone for the entrance gate symbolically reflecting as a "Gateway To Knowledge" - which was renamed as "General B.C. Joshi Dwar." General Joshi was instrumental in initiating civil-military dialogue and created an endowment fund from the Indian Army to establish a Chair in Policy Studies and himself suggested the name of the Chair as Chhatrapati Shivaji Chair in Policy Studies, and instituted the Resident Scholars Programme for the serving Officers of the Indian Army to undertake research on National Security Affairs at the Department of Defense and Strategic Studies Savitribai Phule Pune University.

On 13th November 1994, five days before he passed away, General Joshi had addressed the Association of Indian Universities Vice-

Chancellors' Conference at the University of Pune where he had declared that the 21st Century will be **India's Century**. In this conference, over 185 Vice-Chancellors from Indian and the Commonwealth countries had participated. Till date, he remains the only Service Chief of the Indian Armed Forces to address such a gathering.

In recognition of Gen Joshi's contribution to higher education and furthering University-Armed Forces interaction programmes at various levels and his sensitivity to the issues of national integration, core values and civilizational preconditions of Indian culture, environmental protection, eco-development and perspectives of decision making in national security affairs, the Headquarters Southern Command and the Savitribai Phule Pune University have jointly instituted an annual lecture series in his honour. In 2005, the Chiefs of Staffs Committee resolved that henceforth the Gen B.C. Joshi Memorial Lecture will be delivered in rotation by the three Service Chiefs.

General B.C. Joshi Memorial Lectures provide an invaluable insight to the India's national security issues and concerns emerging in the current security dynamics. By embracing comprehensive analysis to the issues, it helps to understand diverse challenges of security and its implications broadly. In this context, the book incorporates shared ideas of all security forces and their expertise on the concerned issues. Over all, the book generates an idea about existing and emerging national security threats in all domains which needs an immediate attention.

Under the emerging scenario that the institutions of higher education like the universities will bridge the gap between the realm of ideas and the domain of public policy and provide the nation state with the capacity to evolve policy relevant options for national security policy making. The area of national security studies has drawn the attention of the academic community in the Indian university under various nomenclatures since 1942. In which, the security studies have become an essential component of various seminars and conferences that are taking place in the Indian universities.

The Department of Defence and Strategic Studies at Savitribai Phule Pune University in this aspect, has emerged as one of the most dynamic departments and renowned nationally and globally. The department was established in 1963 as the Department of Military Studies, offering undergraduate courses on military studies. In 1974 the department started post-graduation courses focusing more on academic and research activities. On the recommendation of Candeth Committee, this discipline has changed the paradigm of teaching and research activity. Subsequently, the name of the department changed from Military Studies to Defence Studies. In 1984 with the expansion of the scope of the discipline, the name of the department was changed to the Department of Defence and Strategic Studies (DDSS). DDSS has expanded its horizon of discipline through research and innovation and has inculcated thought-provoking teaching. Since its inception, DDSS has been building up institutional knowledge about various aspects of India's national security. As the department shares a strong bond with the Indian Armed Forces, the Chhatrapati Shivaji Chair has been established in Policy Studies by the Indian army in 1994. Chhatrapati Shivaji Chair is a first ever chair established in India by Department of Defence and Strategic Studies, Savitribai Phule University, dedicated to Chhatrapati Shivaji Maharaj. Department of Defence and Strategic Studies (DDSS) and the Indian Air Force (IAF) Headquarters signed Memorandum of Understanding on 29th February 2020 to establish the first ever Chair of Excellence in India, in the name of Marshal of the Indian Air Force Arjan Singh DFC and the second being an Memorandum of Understanding for Resident Scholar Programme (RSP) for Air Force officers, at DDSS, Department is also going to signed Memorandum of Understanding with Indian Navy to initiate Resident Scholar Program in the field of Maritime Security. By taking into account the dedication of the department, Savitribai Phule Pune University has conferred the Best Department Award -2019 to DDSS.

Apart from MA/MSc regular course in Defence and Strategic Studies department is starting new nine Post Graduate Diplomas, One Five Year Integrated Course and one MA program from the academic year 2020-2021.

The department has introduced first ever Post Graduate Diploma in India in the name of great Maratha Worrier Chhatrapati Shivaji Maharaj to disseminate his ideas, thoughts and his extraordinary military tactics and war strategies on nation building process. To understand the war doctrine and strategies adopted during the time of Chhatrapati Shivaji Maharaj and its relevance in the present times the Department of Defence and Strategic studies has initiated the first ever Post Graduate Diploma in India in Chhatrapati Shivaji Maharaj's Vision & Nation Building. This course will provide an overview of strategic thinkers from ancient till Chhatrapati Shivaji Maharaj's period and introduce students to the major strategies of wars and Military organisations of major strategic thinkers like Chhatrapati Shivaji Maharaj, Sun Tzu, Napoleon Bonaparte and Julius Caesar etc.

The Department offers Nine Post- Graduate Diplomas namely P.G. Diploma in Chhatrapati Shivaji Maharaj's Vision & Nation Building, Disaster Management and National Security, Counter Terrorism Studies, Defence Analyst and National Security, West Asia and South Asian Security, African Peace and Security, Chemical, Biological, Radiological, Nuclear & National Security (CBRN), European Peace and Security and Cyber Security and India's National Security and new Master program in Global Peace, Security and Strategies Studies to develop Strategic Culture among Indian Youths. Moreover, it also offers Scholars in Residence Programme under which several officers from the Indian Army and Indian Air Force join the department as visiting scholars.

General B.C. Joshi Memorial Lecture series which began in 1995, has brought together an array of distinguished Service Chiefs from the Armed Forces, a constitutional expert, a governor of state, and a defence minister to come to the University and share their thoughts and concerns about national security issues. The speakers delivered all lectures when they actively held their constitutional positions in the government. The methodology adopted by each of the speakers was based on their perceptions and long experiences on matters related to security. The distinguished speakers have been candid to critically examining the role of the private sector, role of the myopic political rivalries, necessity to establish co-coordinated efforts for national development and defense preparedness, ineffective management of national security, need to define ethics as enlightened self-interest, examine the ambivalent attitudes to national security and defence expenditure and the absolute essentiality to take a long-term view of our national security.

On the occasion of Silver Jubilee of General B. C. Joshi Memorial Lecture, we would like to compile all lectures and publish in a book form from 1994 to 2020. Earlier in 2006, Professor Gautam Sen edited and brought out in-house publication up to 2006. We are continuing the tradition of the department and publishing a book in the name of General B. C. Joshi Memorial Lecture on India's National Security.

This book consists of fifteen speeches and each of the speech focuses on contemporary challenges to national, regional and global security environment which include India's national security, geostrategic concerns, emerging challenges in Indian Ocean Region, Indo-Pacific context and maritime security.

Admiral Karambir Singh (2019) describes contemporary and historical significance of the Indian Ocean Region. He discussed that unique position of India in the Indian Ocean have stimulated maritime activities since the Indus Valley Civilisation. He has also articulated the idea of security and explained maritime security issues which stand on our liberty to promote and achieve national interests. The Indian Navy's role to become a net security provider in the region, counter maritime security challenges to ensure maritime interest and close watch on the evolving security dynamics and their implications on India's maritime security are dealt in a comprehensive manner.

General Bipin Rawat (2017) explains India's national security issues, policies, national security aim and objectives, trust deficits and security environment. He provides a larger perspective of security by covering global security aspect, regional security environment and India's security dilemma under current emerging geostrategic construct. He particularly focuses on China and Pakistan's contested claims over India's territory and proxy war against India and sees recent standoff as China's attempt to change the status quo. He also deals with the internal security challenges and threats which include proxy war, Left wing extremism, Insurgency in North East, Hybrid threats and non-traditional security challenges growing threats to critical infrastructure, national grids and networks from cyber and outer space. He further describes the other significant challenges such as drug trafficking, illegal migration, fake currency, human trafficking and issue of climate change as significant challenges that would remain at the forefront of national response strategy. He concludes that to pursue the national objectives contain diplomacy, economic power and military power.

Air Chief Marshal Arup Raha (2015) mainly focuses on the transformation of the Indian Air Force (IAF) in terms of the challenges and opportunities and considers certain relevant aspects of military power in general. He elucidates evolution of military power which determined by the strength of its army or land forces and historically the great powers have demonstrated mastery over creation, deployment and use of military power to achieve their national objectives. He opines military power is the most important component and economic potential comes as second in the comprehensive national power. He finally discusses the IAFs core competency in exploitation of aerospace power exclusively its offensive capability which remain the prime instrument of military power.

Admiral D.K. Joshi (2013) highlights the key contributions of Indian Navy in the journey of nation's progress and prosperity. He believes development and national security are both sides of same coin. The idea of comprehensive security and comprehensive national strength emerged with the globalisation and economic integration goes beyond military dimensions and economic, societal, energy and environmental security is inter-linked and gaining economic prosperity and social development are centered on it. He anticipates India's fortune are tremendously lies in the seas and Navy as a maritime power contributes to the nation's quest for prosperity by enabling creation of a peaceful periphery to facilitate socio-economic growth.

Lt. Gen. A.K. Singh (2012) discusses perspective on war in the 21st century which has changed in all spheres of human affairs and largely determined by information technology not prevailed earlier. He explains changing nature of conflict and trends, dynamics, characteristics of future conflict, role of air power, maritime power and nuclear dimension. He further debates that in the past war and threats were closely related to statecraft which made states to identify the adversaries and prepare accordingly which is not the case in 21st century where it has become difficult to quantify and identify the threats. Therefore, he suggests identifying trends is important to meet those challenges effectively.

General Deepak Kapoor (2009) defines India's national security challenges in the next decade by highlighting issues related to national security perspective, threats to national security and management of national security. He believes India's strategic location, size and population provides an immense opportunity to play significant role and growing close relationship with other countries also encourages towards taking larger responsibility in the emerging global order.

Air Chief Marshal F.H. Major (2008) examines the emergence of the Indian Air Force as a Strategic Aerospace Power, strategic nature of Air

Power, contribution of Aerospace Power and major influences governing geopolitical environment. He views conflicts in the future are likely to be short, sharp which would be conducted at all levels and against a variety of objectives. He articulates that geo-political compulsions, economic and political realities, foreign policy and national will dictate the growth of aerospace power and a nation's aerospace capability undoubtedly form one of the major strands of strategic posture. He further suggests that there is a need of thorough understanding about the principles of airpower and its applications.

Air Chief Marshal S.P. Tyagi (2005) shares views on the role of the IAF in the changing regional security environment. He largely focuses on geopolitical and security environment, South Asian the Indian Ocean Region, threat assessment, India's response, the role of Indian Air force in the security matrix, its involvement in the wars since independence and current achievements. He sees the strength and credibility of IAF in the present context as a powerful deterrent to any hostile design.

Admiral Arun Prakash (2004) analyses the maritime dimension of national security, the Indian Ocean region and India's maritime past, India's maritime interests, the strategic scenario, relevance of navy and emerging trends of research in the field of national security in developed countries and India. In which, universities and industrial houses are willingly investing intellectual and financial resources for conducting research on national security issues as security matrix currently include economy, environment and from weapons to war. He argues that to become a true maritime power, it is vital for people to have maritime temperament and outlook and need to focus more seawards than inwards plays significant role in decision making or political level of security planning.

George Fernandes (2002) observes the concept of national security and highlights India's ideological concepts of peace, non-violence and rectitude. He defines rectitude as dharma applicable to individuals and institutions and adherence of the spirit of dharma between the relationships of states directs towards shanti of equitable peace forms the conceptual foundation of comprehensive security in Indian matrix. He further argues that all states are amoral and pursue what serves their self- interest best and views strategic convergences of India and the United States an ethical choice which he terms as enlightened self-interest.

General K.V. Krishna Rao (2000) stresses Kashmir: past, present and future. He argues Kashmir as not only an internal issue but also a problem with international ramifications and poses serious security and integrity challenges to India due to its great strategic significance. The General further contends that it is essential to understand the key developments of the past and present situations and visualise the potential future consequence. He recommends that an effective organisation must take shape in order to protect and promote India's vital interests and secure it from being endangered.

Air Chief Marshal A.Y. Tipnis (1999) gives emphasis on Indigenous Science and Technology in the Shaping of Air Power for National Security. He provides wider understanding about national security by explaining extended definition of national security and its framework. He asserts that national security calls on the state and citizen not only to safeguard the existing way of life but also to uplift it to a higher quality and reducing personal risk in everyday life. He further explicates technical sciences, technology, together with human and sociological sciences must be applied in equal measure for the development of human resources, strengthening of national life, promotion of harmony, eradication of poverty and healing of fissiparous forces which is tend to be think only in technical process. He broadly argues for co-ordinate effort for national development and defence preparedness and identifying strength and weaknesses of various agencies to secure India's future in 21st century.

General Shankar Roy Chowdhary (1998) argues that India's national well-being and security highly depends on economic prosperity, social stability and national security constitutes national power. He analyses economic progress of India made so far and argues economic prosperity alone is not sufficient for true prosperity which also requires social content and needs to introspect over the political systems. He critically examines the India's progress on economic, social and political domain and articulates that it is need to go back to our roots to revival of the human values and principles of our freedom struggle and national renaissance must be placed at top.

Shri Nani A. Palkhivala (1995) describes divisiveness as disease emerged in India spreading fast in the people's mind which is communal hatred, linguistic fanaticism, and regional loyalty. He contemplates unity as vital for India's survival and claims national integration is born in the hearts of the citizens and when it dies there, no army, no government and no constitution can save it. He believes the very heart of our national integration lies in the consciousness of the essential unity of all religions and inter-faith harmony which is at stake.

General B.C. Joshi (1994) describes role of universities towards the armed forces by emphasising concerns and aspirations about the involvement of citizens, academia and military in national security and in national development. He also critically examines the research publications on ancient security doctrine. Finally, he argues that no country really has prospered which has ignored its soldier.

Considering the contents of these deliberations we have added the address of late General B.C. Joshi, which he delivered at the University of Pune, merely five days before he passed away. It is a curtain raiser in terms of assessment of India's role in the 21st century. The B.C. Joshi Memorial Lectures delivered over the past twenty five years have all validated the same notions and hence form an important document to be reflected upon by scholars, experts and researchers in future. We consider it a privilege to be given the opportunity to edit this volume and NISDA to publish the same on behalf of the department of Defence and Strategic Studies Savitribai Phule Pune University.

Savitribai Phule Pune University wish to record sincere thanks and gratitude to the eminent contributors who have delivered the yearly General B. C. Joshi memorial Lectures since 1995 at the University. The publication of this edited book would not have been possible without the encouragement and support of the former Vice-Chancellors, Heads of the Department of Defence and Strategic Studies, Prof. Gautam Sen, Prof. Shrikant Parnajpe, and Prof. Arun Dalvi and all university authorities who are continuously supporting for this important task. We are also thankful to the Staff of Southern Command for all administrative and other support for organizing lectures every year.

Finally, we thank the teaching and non-teaching staff of the DDSS, Dr. Ravi Thorat, Dr. Deepali Khaire, Dr. Anjani Devi, Mr. P.J. Khache, Dr. Sushma Bhosale, Dr. Tanvi Kulkarni, Dr. Savita Patil, Ms. Raisa Chaudhary, Ms. Bharathi Kokil, Dr. Dimple Chaudhary, Mr. Balaji Kambale, Ms. Shivani S. Singh, Mr. Satish Gadadare, Mr. Sagar Gaikwad, Ms. Sheetal Jagtap, Mr. Dnyaneshwar Gaikwad, Mr. Gaurav Kokil,

Mr. Onkar Sonwane, Mr. Vijay Mohad, Mr. Ganesh Shinde, Mr. B. Munnuswami and all serving officers, who are students and research scholars in the department who helped us a lot in completing this book.

We are thankful to Mr. Rajan Arya and his team from Pentagon Press LLP for bringing out the book within the shortest possible time. We hope that the readers will find out our efforts worthy and the book will serve the expected needs.

Prof. (Dr.) Nitin R. Karmalkar
Prof. (Dr.) Vijay S. Khare

About the Contributors

Admiral Karambir Singh, PVSM, AVSM, ADC, Chief of the Naval Staff

Admiral Karambir Singh assumed command of the Indian Navy on 31 May 2019, as the 24th Chief of the Naval Staff.

Admiral Karambir Singh is an alumnus of the National Defence Academy, Khadakwasla. Commissioned into the Indian Navy in July 1980, he earned his wings as a helicopter pilot in 1981 and has flown extensively on Chetak (Alouette) and Kamov helicopters. He is a graduate of the Defence Services Staff College, Wellington; College of Naval Warfare, Mumbai, and has served as Directing Staff in both these institutions.

In his career spanning over 39 years, he has commanded the Indian Coast Guard ship *Chandbibi*, missile corvette INS *Vijaydurg*, as well as two guided missile destroyers, INS *Rana* and INS *Delhi*. He has also served as the Fleet Operations Officer of the Western Fleet. Ashore, he has served at Naval Headquarters as the Joint Director Naval Air Staff, and as Captain Air and Officer-in-Charge of the Naval Air Station at Mumbai. He has also served as member of the Aircrew Instrument Rating and Categorisation Board (AIRCATS).

On promotion to flag rank, the Admiral was appointed as the Chief of Staff, Eastern Naval Command. His other important flag appointments include Chief of Staff of the Tri-Services Unified Command at Andaman and Nicobar Islands and Flag Officer Commanding, Maharashtra and Gujarat Naval Area (FOMAG).

In the rank of Vice-Admiral, he has been Director-General of Project Seabird, in-charge of infrastructure development of the Navy's expansive and modern base at Karwar. At the Integrated Headquarters Ministry of Defence (Navy), the Admiral has been the Deputy Chief of Naval Staff and, subsequently, the Vice-Chief of Naval Staff. He was the Flag Officer Commanding-in-Chief, Eastern Naval Command at Visakhapatnam, prior to taking over the helm as the Chief of the Naval Staff on 31 May 2019.

The Admiral enjoys cycling, running, swimming and golf.

Gen Bipin Rawat, UYSM, AVSM, SM, VSM, COAS Chief of Army Staff

General Bipin Rawat is an alumnus of St. Edward School, Shimla, and the National Defence Academy, Khadakwasla; he was commissioned to the Fifth Bn, the Eleventh Gorkha Rifles of the Indian Army in December 1978, from IMA, Dehradun, where he was awarded the 'Sword of Honour'. The officer has vast experience in operations across a wide spectrum of conflict and terrain profiles. He commanded an Infantry battalion along the Line of Actual Control in the Eastern Sector; a Rashtriya Rifles sector; an Infantry Division in the Kashmir Valley; and a Corps in the North-east. The officer also commanded a Multinational Brigade, in a Chapter VII mission in the Democratic Republic of Congo (MONUC). As an Army Cdr, he commanded a theatre of ops along the Western Front.

General Rawat's staff and instructional assignments include an Instructional tenure at IMA Dehradun; General Staff Officer at the Military Operations Directorate; Logistics staff officer of a Division in Central India; Colonel Military Secretary and Deputy Military Secretary in the Military Secretary's Branch; and Senior Instructor, Junior Command Wing. He has been Major General, General Staff of the Eastern Theatre, and the Vice-Chief of the Army Staff.

General Bipin Rawat is a graduate of the Defence Services Staff College, Wellington, the Higher Command and National Defence College courses and has attended the Command and General Staff Course at Fort Leavenworth, USA. The officer during the span of over 38 years service in uniform has been awarded for gallantry and distinguished service with the UYSM, AVSM, YSM, SM, VSM; COAS Commendation on two occasions and the Army Commander's Commendation. Whilst serving with the United Nations, he was twice awarded the Force Commander's Commendation.

Academically inclined, the General has authored numerous articles on 'National Security' and 'Leadership', which have been published in various journals and publications. He was awarded M. Phil. in Defence Studies from Madras University, and holds two diplomas in Management and Computer Studies, respectively. General Bipin Rawat completed his research on military media strategic studies and was awarded Doctorate of Philosophy (Ph.D.) from Chaudhary Charan Singh University, Meerut.

The General Officer assumed the appointment of the Chief of the Army Staff on 31 Dec 2016.

Air Chief Marshal Arup Raha, PVSM, VM, ADC, Chairman, Chief of Staff Committee and Chief of Air Staff

Air Chief Marshal Arup Raha, PVSM, AVSM, VM, ADC graduated from the National Defence Academy, Pune, with the President's Gold Medal in 1973 and was commissioned in the Flying Branch in December 1974. Air Chief Marshal Raha is an experienced fighter pilot. He is a Cat A Qualified Flying Instructor and a Fighter Combat Leader with nearly 3,400 hrs of flying experience, mainly on fighter aircraft. He has served as a Directing Staff at two premier institutes of the IAF, Flying Instructors School and the Tactics and Combat Development Establishment. He has functioned as an inspector in the Directorate of Air Staff Inspection in Air Headquarters and as Staff Officer to the Chief of the Air Staff. He was deputed as the Military and Air Attaché in the Embassy of India, Kyiv, Ukraine from 1999 to 2001. He has held many operational assignments such as Commanding Officer of a MiG-29 Squadron, Station Commander of Air Force Station, Bhatinda, in Punjab during 'OP PARAKRAM', Air Officer Commanding, Air Force Station, Adampur, and Advance Headquarters Western Air Command, Chandi Mandir. He has also served as the Deputy Commandant, Air Force Academy, Hyderabad and Senior Air Staff Officer at Headquarters, Western Air Command. He has the rare distinction of being the Air Officer Commanding in Chief of two Operational Commands, i.e., Central Air Command and the Western Air Command. Before taking over as Chief of the Air Staff, he held the appointment of Vice-Chief of the Air Staff. He is currently the Commodore Commandant of No. 47 Squadron. Air Chief Marshal Raha is an alumnus of Defence Services Staff College and the National Defence College, Delhi. For his distinguished service, he has been awarded Param Vishisht Seva Medal, Ati Vishisht Seva Medal and Vayu Sena Medal. He was appointed as Honorary Aide-de-Camp (Air) to the Hon'ble President of India wef 01 December 2012. Air Chief Marshal Raha is married to Lily Raha and has two children. He is an avid reader and a keen golfer who enjoys travelling.

Admiral D.K. Joshi, PVSM, AVSM, YSM, NM, VSM, ADC, Chief of the Naval Staff

Admiral Devendra Kumar Joshi took over from Admiral Nirmal Verma on August 31 as the 21st Chief of Naval Staff of Independent India and is the 19th Indian to take command of the Indian Navy.

In the morning, Admiral Joshi paid tribute to the country's martyrs by laying a wreath at the Amar Jawan Jyoti and inspected an impressive Guard of Honour on the lawns of South Block. Later, in the office of the CNS, Adm. Nirmal Verma ceremonially handed over the Chief's telescope to Admiral D.K. Joshi.

In his maiden message to the Navy, he said he was "in gratitude for having been given the honour and privileged opportunity to command the Navy" and indicated his priorities as the new Naval Chief. He stated it is "for the Navy to fulfil its mandate as a maritime power for national prosperity, 24 x 7 attention would need to be paid at all levels to ensure that there are no gaps in our security preparedness". He emphasised that "to achieve security related objectives, the man-machine interface is crucial and the Navy would need to professionally re-audit, train and consolidate its preparedness to optimize the existing capabilities as well as harness the full potential of the transformational new capabilities being inducted".

Admiral D.K. Joshi is a specialist in Anti-Submarine Warfare. In his long and distinguished service spanning nearly 38 years, he has served in a variety of Command, Staff and Instructional appointments. Admiral Joshi's Sea Commands include guided missile corvette INS *Kuthar*, guided missile destroyer INS *Ranvir* and the aircraft carrier INS *Viraat*, for which he was awarded Nau Sena Medal, Vishist Seva Medal and Yudh Seva Medal, respectively. He subsequently commanded the Eastern Fleet, wherein he was awarded Ati Vishist Seva Medal (AVSM).

After his elevation to Flag rank, the Admiral served in the Integrated Headquarters in all nodal branches. In the Personnel Branch as the Assistant Chief of Personnel (Human Resource Development), in Warship Production and Acquisition as the Assistant Controller of the Aircraft Carrier Programme (ACCP), and thereafter in the Operations Branch, both as Assistant Chief of Naval Staff (Information Warfare and Operations) and as the Deputy Chief of Naval Staff.

Before taking over as the FOC-in-C Western Naval Command, he contributed towards inter-Service integration, first as the Commander-in-Chief of the Andaman and Nicobar Command, the only tri-service integrated Command. He was awarded the Param Vishist Seva Medal (PVSM) during this time. Later, he served as the Chief of Integrated Defence Staff to Chairman, Chiefs of Staff Committee (CISC).

Admiral Joshi is a distinguished graduate of the Naval War College, USA, an alumnus of the College of Naval Warfare, Mumbai, and the prestigious National Defence College, New Delhi. He was also the Defence Advisor in the Indian High Commission at Singapore from 1996 to 1999.

He is married to Chitra Joshi and the couple have two daughters.

Lt Gen A.K. Singh, PVSM, AVSM, ADC, GOC-in-C, Southern Comd.

Lt. General Ajay Kumar Singh. PVSM, AVSM, SM, VSM (Retd.) is the former Lieutenant Governor of Andaman and Nicobar Islands. He is an alumnus of Sainik School, Rewa and National Defence Academy. He is former Commander in Chief of Southern Command of Indian Army.

Singh was named the 11th Lieutenant Governor of Andaman and Nicobar Islands in July 2013 and took office on 8 July 2013. He was given the additional responsibility of the administration of Puducherry from July 2014 to May 2016.

Singh is known for his contributions towards Andaman society by starting Andaman's first medical college, ANIMERS and second degree college of South Andaman, ANCOL.

Singh left the Andaman and Nicobar Islands after handing over charges on 19 August 2016.

Gen Deepak Kapoor, PVSM, AVSM, SM, VSM, ADC, Chief of Army Staff

General Deepak Kapoor, PVSM, AVSM, SM, VSM, ADC was commissioned from the Indian Military Academy into the Indian Army and the Regiment of Artillery on 11 June 1967. He took over as the Chief of Army Staff on 30 September 2007 and as Chairman, Chiefs of Staff Committee, on 31 August 2009.

In a distinguished career spanning over four decades, he has held important command and staff appointments. The General Officer has taken an active part in the Indo-Pak War of 1971 in the operations for the liberation of Bangladesh. As Commanding Officer of 74 Medium Regiment, he oversaw its conversion from heavy mortars to medium guns. His performance as Chief Operations Officer for all United Nations forces deployed in Somalia was recognized with the award of the Vishisht Seva Medal.

Besides commanding a Line of Control Mountain Brigade in Jammu & Kashmir for which he was awarded the Sena Medal, he has steered an Infantry Division, which is part of the Strike Corps, during mobilization of the Indian Army on the Western borders in Operation PARAKRAM. The General Officer was conferred the Ati Vishisht Seva Medal for his inspiring command of a Corps deployed on the Indo-China border in the Northeast.

On promotion as Army Commander, he initially commanded the Army Training Command, and then the Northern Command. His strategic guidance and astute handling led to stabilization of the situation in the State of Jammu & Kashmir, which was recognized, with the award of the Param Vishisht Seva Medal. Prior to his present appointment, he has served as Vice Chief of Army Staff. He has been appointed Honorary ADC to the Honourable President of India.

The General Officer has schooled at Sainik School, Kunjpura, and is an alumnus of National Defence Academy, Defence Services Staff College and National Defence College. He has an abiding interest in self-education, self-improvement and acquisition of knowledge. He is an excellent sportsman and has played hockey, basketball, tennis and golf at various levels. The General Officer retired on 30 March 2010.

Air Chief Marshal F.H. Major, PVSM, AVSM, SC, VSM, ADC, Chief of Air Staff

Air Chief Marshal Fali Homi Major was born on 29 May 1947 in Secunderabad. He studied at Wesley High School, Secunderabad and was commissioned in the Indian Air Force on 31 December 1967.

The Air Chief Marshal has flown over 7,000 hours on various aircraft and helicopters. As a Wing Commander, he commanded the IAFs first Mi-17 Squadron, which operated at the Siachen Glacier, the world's highest battlefield. As a Group Captain, he commanded another Mi-17 Squadron, leading it into battle during the operations of the Indian Peacekeeping Force in Sri Lanka. For his leadership and courage during this tenure, he was awarded the Vayu Sena Medal (Gallantry). Later, as Station Commander of Air Force Station, Sarsawa, he led the daring rescue of eleven passengers from a stranded cable car in the middle of a valley in Himachal Pradesh. For this act of gallantry, he was awarded the Shaurya Chakra.

He has held a number of other important staff and field appointments including Joint Director (Helicopter Operations) and Director Operations (Transport & Helicopters). In 1999, he took over as the Air Officer Commanding Leh (Ladakh) in the aftermath of the Kargil conflict. For his leadership, successful accomplishment of tasks and distinguished service of a very high order, he was awarded the Ati Vishist Seva Medal by the President of India in January 2002. He was promoted to the rank of Air Vice-Marshal in February 2002 and appointed as Assistant Chief of the Air Staff (Personnel Airmen & Civilians) at Air Headquarters. On promotion to the rank of Air Marshal on January 4, he moved to HQ Integrated Defence Staff as the Deputy Chief of Integrated Defence Staff, Operations and directed the relief, rescue and rehabilitation operations of the Indian Armed Forces in India and abroad in the aftermath of the tsunami. On 5 September 2005, he was appointed as the Air Officer Commanding-in-Chief, Eastern Air Command. That tenure saw the successful conduct of three major international air exercises with the United States Air Force, Republic of Singapore Air Force and the French Air Force. He was awarded the Param Vishisht Seva Medal by the President of India on 26 January 2006.

He is a graduate of the National Defence College and Army War College. He is married to Zareen and they have two children. His son is a pilot with Jet

Airways. His daughter is married and is a homemaker. The Air Chief Marshal is an avid golfer and cricket fan.

Air Chief Marshal S.P. Tyagi, PVSM, AVSM, VSM, ADC, Chief of Air Staff

Air Chief Marshal Shashindra Pal Tyagi became the 20th Chief of Air Staff on 31 December 2001. He was commissioned as a fighter pilot in the Indian Air Force on 31 December 1963. He has the distinction of having flown several types of fighter and transport aircraft and has logged over 3,000 flying hours. His combat experience includes Combat Air Patrols as well as Strike and interdiction missions during the 1965 Indo-Pak War. In the 1971 War, he flew MiG-21 aircraft on Air Defence missions.

He has held a number of important field appointments, which include Commanding Officer of a Jaguar squadron and the Air Officer Commanding, Air Force Station, Jamnagar. As the Defence Attaché in Saudi Arabia, he had a first-hand view of Operation Desert Storm. He has held many important staff appointments including Director Air Defence, Assistant Chief of the Air Staff (Intelligence), Assistant Chief of the Air Staff (Operations) at Air Headquarters and Senior Air Staff Officer, HQ Central Air Command. He has been the Air Officer Commanding-in-Chief of three Operational Commands—the Central, South-Western and the Western Air Command. Air Chief Marshal Tyagi took over as the Chairman, Chiefs of Staff Committee, on 31 October 2006.

The Air Chief is fond of the outdoors and keeps himself fit. He holds the distinction of being the first ever to have earned para wings as Chief. He is a current and enthusiastic sky-diver. He functions through delegation, is a people's man and a captivating orator. He is the recipient of the Presidential awards of Param Vishist Seva Medal, Ati Vishist Seva Medal and Vayu Sena Medal for his exemplary leadership and distinguished service.

He is married to Vandana, they have a son, Anurag, and a daughter, Rasika. Air Chief Marshal S.P. Tyagi retired on 31 March 2007, handing over the charge to Air Chief Marshal F.H. Major.

Admiral Arun Prakash, PVSM, AVSM, VRC, VSM, Naval Chief and Chairman, Chiefs of Staff

Admiral Arun Prakash, PVSM, AVSM, VrC, VSM (Retd) served as India's 20th Naval Chief and Chairman, Chiefs of Staff. An aviator by specialisation, during his 40-year career, he commanded a carrier-borne fighter squadron, a naval air station and four warships; including the aircraft carrier INS *Viraat*. He has also logged over 2,500 hours in fighters, patrol aircraft and helicopters. In flag rank, he commanded the Eastern Fleet, the National Defence Academy, the Andaman & Nicobar Joint Command and the Western Naval Command. On staff, he served as the head of the Aviation and Personnel Branches of the Navy and as the Vice-Chief of Naval Staff. During his tenure at the helm, the Navy saw many initiatives being launched in the fields of doctrine, strategy, transformation and foreign maritime cooperation. He is a graduate of the IAF Test Pilots' School, Defence Services Staff College and the US Naval War College. During the 1971 War, he was awarded the Vir Chakra while flying with an IAF fighter squadron in the Punjab. Post-retirement, he served two terms as a member of the National Security Advisory Board and was Chairman of the National Maritime Foundation. He served on the 1999 Arun Singh Task force as well as the Naresh Chandra Committee on national security reforms. He lives in Goa and writes and speaks on strategic and security related topics. The Admiral holds the distinguished Chair at a college and is the guiding light for research carried out by faculty and course participants.

George Fernandes, Former Defence Minister, India

George Fernandes served as Defence Minister between 1998 and 2004. He was one of the most prominent leaders of the socialist movement in the 1970s and a senior Janata Dal leader before founding the Samata Party by himself. He is well known for his larger role during emergency in India. Besides defence ministry, during the Atal Bihari Vajpayee-led government, Mr Fernandes held several ministerial portfolios include communications, industry and railways. In 1999, when the Kargil war broke out, he paid a record

32nd visit to the world's highest battle field at Siachen glacier in 2003. Mr Fernandes made it a point to visit the glacier every six months to see the induction of new units to guard the inhospitable mountains during his period. Since 2009-2010, he served as a parliamentarian in Rajya Sabha.

General K.V. Krishna Rao, PVSM, Chief of the Army Staff

General Krishna Rao was born on 16 July 1923, and was educated in Maharaja's College, Vizianagaram, Andhra Pradesh. He completed his military training at Officers Training School, Bangalore, and was commissioned into 2 Mahar on 9 August 1942. For a short while, the unit was employed on internal security duties at Nagpur during the Quit India Movement. During the Second World War, he served in the North West Frontier, Baluchistan, and Burma.

After the war, he was selected for a permanent commission as well as for the civil service. He opted for the Army. He took part in the 1947-48 War in Jammu & Kashmir (J&K). He attended Defence Services Staff College, commanded 3 Mahar, and was posted as instructor at the Staff College in March 1963. In 1967, he was selected for studies at the Imperial Defence College in the UK. He took over command of 26 Infantry Division in 1969.

He had just completed about a year in this job when he was shifted to 8 Mountain Division in Nagaland in September 1970. The situation in Nagaland and Manipur had deteriorated, and the Army Chief had specially selected him for this task. The rebel Naga groups fighting for independence were getting arms aid from Pakistan and China. The security forces were compelled to act against the underground movement. Gen. Krishna Rao improved the Intelligence system and ensured that the local population was not alienated. Any allegations of excess by troops was investigated and action taken when necessary. This ensured good relations with the locals and the state government.

In the 1971 Indo-Pak War, the Division secured Sylhet. The Pakistani troops fought hard, but were pushed back. They offered to surrender on 16 December and were assured treatment as per the Geneva Convention. They were apprehensive of revenge attacks by Mukti Bahini soldiers and were allowed to keep their arms until the Indian troops were available in strength to ensure their safety. The Division received orders to move back to Nagaland in January, General Krishna Rao was awarded the PVSM for outstanding leadership, courage, determination and drive. On his return to Nagaland, General Krishna Rao took the initiative to reach out to the hostile force and a meeting was held with the underground "Home Minister Subeto". The meeting scheduled for thirty minutes went on for four hours. He left on posting to Shimla in end May 1972, and subsequently an agreement did materialise with the hostile party.

He was appointed as Chief of Army Staff on 1 June 1981, and met Prime Minister (PM) Indira Gandhi regularly, and put across his views frankly. She consulted him on various issues concerning internal security. He found that the threat had been underestimated in some sectors and updated the operational plans. He retired on 31 July 1983. His services were warmly recognised by the PM who wanted him to stay on in Delhi as advisor. But he retired to his home in Hyderabad and declined job offers from the CM of Andhra Pradesh and a few companies. He accepted the offer of an assignment as Governor of Nagaland, Manipur and Tripura in June 1984.

The area was beset with secessionist movements, insurgency, political instability and ineffective administration. At one stage, President's Rule had to be imposed in Nagaland. He took steps to tone up the administration, visited all the districts and reached out to the political leaders.

The PM then invited him to take over the governorship of J & K. Insurgency had broken out there. He was sworn in as Governor of J & K on 11 July 1989. Vested interests made false allegations against him in that he favoured the Congress. V.P. Singh had taken over as PM and he offered his resignation, which was accepted on 18 January 1990. When a proxy war developed in J & K and reached its peak, he was re-appointed as Governor and served there from 12 March 1993 to 1 May 1998. In this capacity, he was instrumental in restoring peace and democracy in the insurgency-driven state after a long gap of seven years. Krishna Rao passed away on 30 January 2016 in New Delhi.

Air Chief Marshal A.Y. Tipnis, AVSM, VM, ADC CAS, Chief of the Air Staff

Anil Yashwant Tipnis was born on 15 September 1940, and did his education at Barnes High School, Deolali. His initiation into the Services started with him joining the 15th Course of the National Defence Academy (NDA) in January 1956, after which he moved on for flying training to the Air Force Flying College in January 1959.

Anil Yashwant Tipnis was commissioned into the Indian Air Force (IAF) as a fighter pilot on 28 May 1960. He finished his training with flying colours, receiving the coveted

Majumdar Trophy for his excellent performance. The initial years of Tipnis' service were spent as an operational pilot in several frontline fighter squadrons.

His first posting was to a Hunter Squadron. In 1963, when Wg. Cdr. Dilbagh Singh (later Air Chief Marshal and CAS of the IAF) raised the first MiG-21 Squadron, Tipnis was one of the few pilots to be sent to No.28 Squadron to fly the MiG-21s. He was still serving with the *First Supersonics* when war broke out in September 1965, and he served with the squadron during its operations in the war.

In 1966, he graduated as a Pilot Attack Instructor (PAI) and won the Naronha Trophy for standing first. This was followed in January 1970 with a deputation to Iraq as a PAI. On return, he was posted as the Flight Commander of No.45 Squadron, which then served as a MiG-21 Operational Conversion Unit. He qualified as a Fighter Combat Leader at the IAF's prestigious Tactics & Air Combat Development Establishment (TACDE) in 1973 winning the Sword of Honour; he continued on staff as a flight commander of the Combat Development & Training Flight.

In 1975, he underwent the Defence Services Staff Course at Wellington following which, in July 1977, he took over as the Commanding Officer of No. 23 Squadron equipped with MiG-21 bis aircraft. Tipnis was one of the four officers short-listed for the Indo-Soviet Joint Space mission. He underwent all the training required for the mission in the course of the final selection. After a couple of staff appointments and a stint at the National Defence Academy as the Chief Instructor (Air) and Battalion Commander, he was posted to France in October 1983 as the Team Leader for the Mirage Project Team in the rank of Group Captain, where he was responsible for the negotiation and purchase of the Mirage 2000 aircraft for the IAF.

On returning to India three years later, he was posted to the Mirage 2000 base of the IAF, as the Air Officer Commanding, Air Force Station, Gwalior, in the rank of Air Commodore. In 1989, he attended the Defence Studies Course at the National Defence College, New Delhi, and successfully completed it. Later, he was posted as Deputy Personnel Officer at Air HQ in New Delhi.

More important staff appointments at Air HQ and Command HQ followed. On promotion to the rank of Air Vice-Marshal in June 1992, he was appointed the Assistant Chief of the Air Staff (Inspection) at Air Headquarters. In June 1993, he took over as the Air Officer Commanding J&K area. On being promoted to the rank of Air Marshal in September 1994, he took over as the Senior Air Staff Officer (SASO) of Eastern Air Command and later, in February 1995, was posted as the SASO of Western Air Command, the largest operational command of the Indian Air Force. In August 1995, he assumed charge as AOC-in-C of Western Air Command. He was appointed as the Vice-Chief of Air Staff (VCAS) in April 1997. On 31 December 1998, he was promoted as Air Chief Marshal and took over as the 18th Chief of Air Staff. Upon his retirement on 31 December 2001, he had completed 41+ years in uniform.

His tenure saw the first deployment of Indian Air Force combat aircraft in action since the 1971 War. When the fighting at Kargil erupted, the IAF was deployed to attack intruders' positions in the high-altitude areas. Needless to say, the IAF acquitted itself very well in these limited actions. Throughout the course of operations, the Air Chief Marshal was deeply involved in overseeing the conduct of operations. Along with the then Army Chief, General V.P. Malik, he visited the frontline units and forward areas to get a feel of the progress of the operations.

Duringhis career in the Air Force, Air Chief Marshal Tipnis received the Param Vishisht Seva Medal, Ati Vishisht Seva Medal and Vayu Sena Medal for distinguished service.

He is keen on outdoor activity and plays golf and tennis regularly. His other outdoor activities include gliding and sailing. His passion for flying continues till today, and he loves being in the cockpit, be it that of a glider, helicopter, transport aircraft and particularly of a fighter. He continued to maintain his currency on fixed wing (fighters and transport aircraft) as well as rotary wing aircraft during his service as Air Chief.

General Shankar Roy Chowdhury, PVSM, ADC, Chief of the Army Staff

General S. Roy Chowdhury, PVSM, ADC, was born on 6 September 1937 at Calcutta and was educated at Calcutta and Mussoorie. He joined the Joint Services Wing, Dehradun, in 1953 and was commissioned into 20 Lancers on 9 June 1957. He participated in the Indo-Pak conflict in 1965 and 1971 including operations for the liberation of Bangladesh. He commanded an Independent Armoured Brigade from December 1980 to July 1983 and Armoured Division from May 1988 to May 1990. He subsequently commanded a Corps in Jammu and Kashmir in 1991-92.

He is a graduate of Defence Services Staff College and held several staff and instructional appointments, including that of Director General Combat Vehicle dealing with the Indian Main Battle Tank 'Arjun'.

Nani A. Palkhivala, Indian Jurist and Liberal Economist

He was a champion of civil liberties, a farsighted economic thinker and a legendary lawyer. Palkhivala joined the chambers of the great Jamshedji Kanga in Bombay. He was also a part-time lecturer in Government Law College, Bombay. He received fame with his advocacy and submissions in the Keshavanand Bharti case in which he persuaded the SC to hold that the power of amendment of the Constitution was not unlimited and could not be exercised so as to damage its basic structure. He also represented India in international forums which includes the special tribunal in Geneva, the International Civil Aviation Organization (Montreal) and World Court (Hague). He is well-known for his famous annual budget speeches and his contribution to Indian constitutional jurisprudence.

For his work he had received a great deal of recognition from academics, academic institutions and the government. In 1977, he was appointed as Indian Ambassador to the United States by the Janata government. He also received honorary doctorates from Princeton University, Rutgers University, Lawrence University, University of Wisconsin–Madison, Annamalai University, Ambedkar Law University and the University of Mumbai.

General B.C. Joshi, PVSM, AVSM, Chief of the Army Staff

General B.C. Joshi, born on 5 December 1935, was commissioned on 4 December 1954 in the 2nd Lancers Regiment of the Armoured Corps. He passed out of the Academy by standing first in the order of merit for which he was awarded the President's Gold Medal. General Joshi, during his career, held important staff and command positions. He commanded an Armoured Regiment in 1971 and was Military, Naval and Air Advisor in the South-Pacific Region from 1973 to 1976. He was the Southern and Western Army Commander between 1990 and 1992, before taking over as the Chief of the Army Staff. He was awarded the Ati Vishisht Seva Medal (AVSM) in 1982 and Param Vishisht Seva Medal (PVSM) in 1991. Kumaon University conferred an Honorary Doctorate on him in March 1994. General Joshi passed away on 18 November 1994, while in office.

In 1995, Headquarter Southern Command and the University of Pune jointly instituted an annual lecture series to honour the memory of General B.C.

Joshi, in recognition of his contribution to higher education and furthering the University and Armed Forces interaction programme. General Joshi was sensitive to the issues of national integration, core values and civilization preconditions of Indian culture, environmental protection, eco-development and perspective of decision-making for national security. In 1998, the University of Pune named one of its gates as General B.C. Joshi Dwar.

General B.C. Joshi Memorial Lectures have been published in the form of a book titled "General BC Joshi Memorial Lectures on National Security", in 2005.

1

Indo-Pacific Changing Dynamics: Maritime Security Imperatives for India

Admiral Karambir Singh,
PVSM, AVSM, ADC,
Chief of the Naval Staff

Salutations

At the outset, let me thank the Vice-Chancellor, Savitribai Phule Pune University, for inviting me to deliver this year's Gen. B.C. Joshi Memorial lecture. I consider being here today a privilege and an honour.

It is well-known that Gen. B.C. Joshi was among the astute military leaders who propagated the thought of 'Scholar-Warrior' and focused on encouraging Army officers to spend time on education and in academic institutions. Rightly so, he was himself honoured with an honorary Doctorate of Science by Kumaon University in 1994. He was also an ardent student of warfare with a deep understanding of national security issues, which enabled him to undertake perceptive and insightful analyses.

I must also put on record that the quality research work and institutional knowledge gained by the Department of Defence and Strategic Studies of this University, over the years, has been a befitting tribute to the Late General. The memorial lecture organized every year by the Department is testimony to the deep association between this University and the Armed Forces.

I must also compliment the University for choosing a pertinent topic for today's talk. 'Maritime Security Challenges in IOR' is indeed a topic of relevance in the current geopolitical situation and is, of course, close to my heart.

Significance of IOR

Before I touch upon what is security...and what security challenges prevail in the IOR, a brief examination of the historical and contemporary significance of the IOR for India would be appropriate.

India's geography has endowed her with all the elements necessary to be a maritime nation. A long coastline, islands territories, and a unique position in the Indian Ocean have encouraged maritime activities along the coast and across the oceans since the times of the ancient Indus Valley civilization. Long before Hippalus, a Greek navigator in the First century BC had disclosed the secret of the 'monsoons 'to the Romans, Indian navigators had been making use of the same winds to explore the seas.

Some of the world's earliest civilizations thrived in regions abutting the Indian Ocean along the Nile, Euphrates, Tigris, Indus and Mekong river basins. These eventually evolved into vibrant societies of West Asia, the Indian subcontinent and South-East Asia. Some of the world's major religions originated in this region and spread to other parts of the world, mainly via sea routes.

The drydock in Lothal in Gujarat, which dates back to 2,200 BC, is testimony to the thriving maritime infrastructure of India, particularly ports of that time. It is from these ports that Indian seafarers sailed to distant lands in Mesopotamia and the East Coast of Africa. The seafaring kingdoms of the Kalingas, the Cholas, the Pandyas and the Cheras, sailed to distant countries in the East and established long lasting trade and cultural links. Even today, cultural evidence of India's maritime outreach is amply evident in all the Southeast Asian countries.

It was, however, during the medieval period and Mughal rule when we lost control over our seas and that paved the way for the entry of seafarers from Europe, starting with the arrival of Vasco da Gama from

Portugal in May 1498 and followed by the Dutch, the British and the French.

The **Maratha Navy's** spirited resistance to European imperialism in the 17th and early 18th centuries, under the able leadership of Chattrapati Shivaji and Sarkhel Konhoji Angre, the admiral of the Marathas, is a glorious chapter in our maritime history. We are indeed privileged to be in the land of the Great Marathas, who were said to be the first and perhaps the only ones to employ a navy against European colonial powers amongst the other Indian states of those times. It is said that "Chattrapati Shivaji Maharaj carried the capital of his empire on the high seas". INS Angre, the naval base at Mumbai, has been so named to immortalize the great admiral of our naval history.

Although the Maratha Navy did contest the European control of our waters, it was not adequate to prevent the establishment of European settlements in India. The key issue that we must always bear in mind is the correlation between the decline in our maritime power and the rise of the primacy of the English East India Company in the Indian Ocean. This lesson of history was articulated by Pandit Jawaharlal Nehru when he famously said, "To be secure on Land, we must be Supreme at Sea".

The sea around us, that is, the Indian Ocean, has always been strategically significant. It is the third largest water body in the world, covering an area of 68.5 million square kilometres. It is surrounded by three continents...38 countries have either coastlines or island territories in this ocean and several more in the hinterland depend on its sea-ways for their national trade. The region hosts around 40 per cent of the global population as well as some of the fastest growing economies of the world.

Additionally, the region also has the largest energy reserves of the world, which are important to nations across the globe. I am sure you must all be aware of the vast petroleum reserves of countries in this region. About 36 million barrels (that is nearly 6 million metric tonnes) of oil is transported every day through the Indian Ocean.

For India, in particular, the dependence on the Indian Ocean is significant, as 90 per cent of international trade by volume and 70 per cent by value come across the seas. Over 82 per cent of India's crude oil requirement is imported, almost exclusively by sea. In addition, over 51 per cent of domestic crude oil production is from off-shore sources within the Indian Exclusive Economic Zone. After considering all the factors, our 'sea dependence' for oil is estimated to be well over 90 per cent. Several Indian companies have invested heavily in the energy sector overseas from Far Eastern Russia to South America and these investments form an important component of the nation's energy security construct. The security of the various energy assets, including supply sources, production infrastructure and means of transportation, has a strong maritime component and is vital to economic progress.

With over 11 million metric tons of fish produced during 2016-17, India is the second largest fish-producing nation in the world. With an annual income of close to US$ 5.8 billion from exports and a huge domestic market, this sector engages approximately 14.5 million people in the country directly and many more along the value chain.

India's merchant ship fleet of around 1,390 ships, adding up to over 19 million Gross Registered Tonnes (GRT), may be modest by global standards, but it is steadily growing. Ably supporting this merchant fleet are 12 major ports and around 200 notified non-major ports dotting our long coastline. In addition, Indian seafarers make up about 6 per cent of the global workforce in the mercantile marine sector.

Given the dependence on the sea for national prosperity, access to and influence over the maritime domain is imperative for a maritime nation like India. Whilst the central location of India offers it a unique advantage by enabling effective monitoring of International Sea Lines, surveillance of the ingress and egress points in the Indian Ocean and adequate maritime reach to the extremities of the Ocean, it also brings with it the daunting task of tackling various 'security threats' across the entire spectrum.

Security

I will dwell a little on the term 'security'. In a sense, it implies an environment that provides freedom from fear and threat, as beautifully expressed so many years ago by Guru Rabindranath Tagore in his famous poem 'Where the mind is without fear'. Security is the existence of that freedom from fear, threat of disruption, division or destruction of our well-being thus creating an environment conducive to the pursuit and development of our core values and interests. 'Maritime security', by extension, pertains to all issues that relate to the seas and bear on our liberty to pursue and promote national interests.

In other words, maritime security entails provision of a secure environment, at and from the seas, that fosters a nation's growth. This maritime environment, however, is influenced by numerous trends and events, such as those we are witnessing now.

As the new world order takes shape, we are seeing several nations jostling for their own space at the high table of world affairs. This desire to claim a greater share in global affairs is one of the key drivers of a gradual transition and possible change of global polarity. In fact, we might also be witnessing a phase in this transition where the conventional understanding of polarities and power block dynamics may need to be reviewed.

These emerging dynamics are largely being played out in the maritime dimension, thereby bringing the maritime domain to the centre stage of world affairs. Countries are building maritime capacities at a hitherto unprecedented scale and rate to project maritime power and enhance security within their desired spheres of influence.

Maritime Security in IOR

In terms of issues relating to security in the IOR, these are best addressed in terms of two overlapping regional systems. The first is specific to the Indian Ocean and its littoral, while the second sees the Indian Ocean as part of a wider Indo Pacific 'strategic system' that embraces a wide geo-strategic construct.

If the Indo-Pacific is viewed as a series of concentric circles, the IOR is its inner core. Hon'ble Prime Minister Narendra Modi defined this region as stretching from the 'shores of Africa to that of the Americas' during the Shangri-la Dialogue on 1 June 2018. He further articulated India's Indo-Pacific policy by emphasising that it stands for having a free, open and inclusive region embracing all nations, within the geography, towards the common pursuit of progress and prosperity and stressed on a 'rule-based international order' towards ensuring security and prosperity in the region.

Whilst the Indo-Pacific is important to us, activities in the Indian

Ocean, our immediate neighbourhood, have a greater impact on our maritime perspective. Maritime trade in the Indian Ocean has always been integral to our economic, cultural and civilizational linkages. The world's preeminent energy and trade seaways and a large percentage of the oil and trade activities (as brought out by me earlier) emanate in the IOR and are headed for countries outside this region. Obviously, the safety, security and stability in the Indian Ocean Region have an extra-regional dimension. Resource competition, energy security and expanding strategic interests are increasing and it is highly likely that the region will continue to occupy the centre stage in times to come, particularly from the perspective of 'competing' interests.

We could possibly be witnessing another period of 'great power transition'. As you are all aware, the leading global power and its competitors are locked in a complex interplay across multiple domains, which include military, technology, economic, climatic and many other issues affecting the strategic environment.

China's rapid growth, Russia's military resurgence and the concurrent perceived decline of US military advantage, are shaping the overall security environment. China, which is increasingly being viewed as a 'peer competitor' to the USA, is now seeking a further departure towards a hierarchical world order. Further, the US-Russia and US-China dynamics have dominated the security discourse at regional and global levels. Emerging fault lines in long-standing arrangements, and the strengthening of new alignments, could well be the initial indications of further disruptions, which, until recently seemed nearly impossible.

The new 'great power politics' has also been made more complex by the rise of regional players. They are asserting themselves to realise their perceived rightful place in the global order and have demonstrated issue-based convergence with different parties.

This power play and competition is accompanied by a shift of the global Centre of Gravity to Asia. While economic, technological and military power is shifting to Asia, numerous historical fault lines in this region still persist. This makes for a complex and uncertain security environment that needs to be carefully monitored.

Compounding the security matrix of the region is the advent of numerous challenges that have come along with increasing globalisation.

The ongoing third wave of globalisation is unprecedented both in pace and intensity, due to the enmeshing of economic and technological developments. A strong desire to sustain economic growth has consequently resulted in a voracious thirst for resources and markets. Nations are exploring avenues far from home, driven by nationalistic as well as economic ambitions. This has aggravated a number of international security issues, some of which are in the maritime domain and have led to new risks and challenges.

These range from traditional challenges, which arise from state-on-state issues as well as a slew of non-traditional challenges. Over the last few decades, these challenges have significantly expanded in diversity and scale.

Whilst the conventional and traditional end of the spectrum continues to be relevant and our major preoccupation, the sub-conventional and non-traditional end of the spectrum has posed equally serious challenges.

Maritime piracy has kept more than 20 navies engaged in the Gulf of Aden since 2008. Human and drug trafficking as well as large-scale illegal, unreported and unregulated (IUU) fishing and poaching leading to adverse economic and ecological consequences for the littorals have also raised alarms in several parts of the world and have kept maritime forces constantly engaged. It has been observed that nations with limited maritime surveillance capabilities, such as some of the IOR island nations, are more likely to be victims of such activity.

All these threats have a hybrid, transnational and non-state character. Often, the illegal activities at sea have their roots across several continents—the flag of the vessel, port of loading and unloading, origin of cargo, nationalities of the crew—all leading to different countries from different corners of the world. The complex nature of the legal process and jurisdiction arising out of such a mix highlights the nature of challenges that beset the maritime domain.

In addition to these challenges, terrorism continues to acquire new dimensions by the day. The reach, access to technology, organisational flexibility and financing avenues that terrorist organisations enjoy today is unprecedented. India has been a victim of State-sponsored terrorism for many years now. Unfortunately, this threat is evolving and is no longer confined to a country or region. It has, in every sense, acquired a global reach and influence. Extremists reportedly receiving underwater attack and deep-sea operations training across the border is one such example of our maritime interests facing an ever-increasing threat.

All these traditional and non-traditional challenges require the Indian Navy to commit substantial effort, resources and continuously evolve strategies for maintaining maritime security in the region. The importance of maritime security for India is further embodied in the words of Shri K.M. Panikkar, India's renowned visionary on maritime affairs, who advocated strongly that *"Unless India is prepared to stand forth and shoulder the responsibility of peace and security in the Indian Ocean, her freedom will mean but little. She will be at the mercy of any power which has the command of the sea"*.

Indian Navy Strategy to Counter Maritime Challenges

Ladies and gentlemen, given the enormity and complexity of the challenges to India's maritime security, the Indian Navy has adopted a multi-dimensional approach to ensure the safety and security in our areas of maritime interest. Since, the area to be guarded at sea has no fences, the force needs flexibility, mobility and visibility. Keeping this in the backdrop, the Indian Navy has, therefore, charted a roadmap to evolve its strategies. I am sure that with such an accredited Department of Defence and Strategic Studies, this audience is familiar with the Indian Maritime Security Strategy.

I will briefly discuss the Indian Navy's strategy for ensuring comprehensive maritime security in a complex and uncertain world.

The Navy's core strategy is built on five pillars. They are strategies for **Deterrence, Conflict, Shaping a Favourable and Positive Maritime Environment, Coastal and Offshore Security, and Maritime Force and Capability Development.**

The foundational pillar of our naval strategy is deterrence against nuclear, conventional and sub-conventional threats. Accordingly, we maintain a credible second-strike nuclear capability as well as a multi-dimensional, combat-ready, conventional maritime force.

Today, as part of **'Mission Based Deployment'** our ships and aircraft are deployed all the way from the Persian Gulf to the Western Pacific almost round the clock. Particularly, in the waters to our West, where our critical energy sea lines of communication exist, our presence has served to deter interference with our interests. During the recent crisis in the Straits of Hormuz, the Indian Navy reacted swiftly and executed **Op Sankalp**. As part of the ongoing operation, the Navy is providing protection to Indian Merchant Marine transiting through the Gulf of Hormuz.

Ladies and gentlemen, we must appreciate the fact that the character of recent conflict has changed significantly. **Technological advancements** have fundamentally changed the ways in which military operations are conducted. Pervasive Intelligence, Surveillance and Reconnaissance networks of satellites, large number of manned and autonomous platforms with multiple sensors, as well as extensive fixed sensor arrays including underwater arrays, have allowed an unprecedented level of battle-space transparency. In addition, use of Artificial Intelligence and data analytics has compressed the timelines of the information-decision-action loop.

These realities are addressed in the second pillar, that is, **'Strategy for Conflict'**. This strategy aims to undertake swift and decisive operations in synergy with the Army and Air Force. This strategy is centred on various operational actions, which include maritime manoeuvre, maritime strike, sea control, sea denial, SLOC interdiction, SLOC protection, coastal and offshore defence, information warfare and escalation management. This application of force to enable termination of conflict on terms favourable to India is done within the ambit of the Laws of Armed Conflict. We also have the sea-based element of our nuclear triad, which is a critical pillar of our nuclear doctrine.

Ladies and gentlemen, what we have been able to operationally achieve across the wide canvas of maritime threats has been largely due to the combat skills honed during exercises and operations at sea. In February this year, for instance, the Navy exercised its composite combat capability through its **Flagship Theatre Level Operational Readiness Exercise, TROPEX**. The exercise saw the participation of all our operational ships, submarines and aircraft, as well as units from the Indian Coast Guard. In addition, significant participation of the Indian Army and Air Force truly enhanced the integrated operations of the three Services.

It was during this exercise that terrorists carried out the dastardly Pulwama attack. The Navy reacted by shifting seamlessly from exercise to coercive deployment. Our carrier battle group, which is an embodiment of reach, sustenance and flexibility, supported by our sub-surface assets and maritime patrol aircraft, were deployed forward in the Arabian Sea to preclude any misadventure in the maritime domain. This is indicative of the flexibility and operational tempo maintained by our forces.

Having spoken about the Indian Navy's strategies to counter traditional challenges, let me now tackle other aspects of maritime security.

In consonance with the Hon'ble Prime Minister's vision of SAGAR, which stands for 'Security And Growth for All in the Region' and 'Neighbourhood First and Act East Policies', the Indian Navy adopts a cooperative approach to meet some of its attendant security priorities. These efforts are guided by the **'Strategy for shaping a Favourable and Positive Maritime Environment'**. The Navy partners other like-minded navies to enhance maritime security in the region through capacity building, training, multinational exercises and providing assistance during natural calamities.

For instance, the Navy assisted Sri Lanka by the concentration of advance Offshore Patrol Vessels, as also Offshore Patrol Vessels and Fast Attack craft for Mauritius. Such resource-sharing has benefited these countries by enhancing their capacity to tackle threats in the maritime domain. Our endeavour is to assist friendly littorals build capacity while inculcating a strong sense of ownership and self-reliance.

On similar lines, our capability enhancement initiatives cover an array of activities, including training, technical support and hydrographic cooperation. On the training front, the Indian Navy covers the entire spectrum of professional military training, ranging from various ab-initio courses to mid-level specialisation, all the way to senior-level courses like the Higher Command course. It is a matter of great pride that we have provided training to over 15,000 trainees from 45 countries till date.

In terms of enhancing security in the region, **Anti-piracy** operations off the Horn of Africa, **Coordinated Patrols** (CORPATS) with countries in the region, and joint **EEZ patrols** for some of our friendly countries based on their requests have helped secure the regions against common maritime threats. Even as we speak, the 73rd anti-piracy deployment of the Indian Navy is in progress in the Gulf of Aden. During the last 11 years, at least one naval ship has continuously maintained its presence in the Gulf of Aden. We have been able to thwart a total of 44 piracy attempts on ships and apprehended more than 120 pirates.

We have further increased our interactions and exercises with foreign navies with the aim of increasing interoperability and sharing best practices. It is our intent to partner with like-minded navies to maintain peace and security over the global commons. This year, we have increased our tempo of maritime exercises with friendly foreign countries with participation in 27 exercises and 04 coordinated patrols.

Our prompt response in rendering Humanitarian Assistance and Disaster Relief to affected regions and the evacuation of a large number of civilians, across nationalities, has demonstrated our commitment to the common good. The Indian Navy has played a yeoman's role in providing relief in times of calamities in the IOR and beyond. This was aptly demonstrated in relief efforts by our forces in Yemen during *Op RAHAT* on April 15, when the Indian Navy safely evacuated over 3,000 civilians, including about 1,300 foreign nationals from 41 different countries, from a live combat zone. In November last year, we evacuated 38 stranded fishermen from the Yemeni Island of Socotra during Cyclone Mekunu. The support rendered by our ships to the people of Mozambique in the aftermath of Cyclone Idai has won accolades from around the world. I am sure many in the audience would recollect images of our helicopters ferrying people to safety and our ships providing on-scene relief to affected people. Through such challenging operations, we have established ourselves as a credible first responder in the wake of any humanitarian emergency or natural disaster in the region.

Moving on, the Indian Navy's foreign cooperation initiatives, such as the Indian Ocean Naval Symposium—IONS and MILAN—the biennial gathering of regional navies have enabled constructive dialogue amongst navies of the Indo-Pacific.

Last year marked the **10th year of IONS** and it is, indeed, heartening to see that this initiative has evolved into a leading maritime organisation of the Indian Ocean Region. The construct has formulated guidelines for

HADR in IOR, which is one of the leading maritime challenges facing the region. In addition, we also conduct table-top exercises followed by actual exercises at sea. For instance, in 2017, we conducted the International Multilateral Maritime Search and Rescue exercise under the leadership of the Bangladesh Navy. This has opened the doors for IONS to graduate from an academic platform to one with greater operational engagement.

We also aim to enhance interoperability between the navies of the region. Last year, the Indian Navy hosted the 10th edition of MILAN at Port Blair with a multilateral exercise, which saw the participation of 20 ships including 11 foreign naval ships, making it the largest multilateral exercise to be conducted in the Andaman Sea. This year, we have invited 41 countries to participate in the 2020 edition of MILAN. This exercise will aim at bringing maritime forces from across the globe together in Visakhapatnam and increase our exercise collaborative efforts at maritime security.

In furthering our commitment to constructive dialogue amongst navies of the Indian Ocean Region, we have started the Goa Maritime Conclave, a congregation of regional heads of navies. This conclave has cemented its place as a forum to seek 'local solutions for local problems'.

While we are consolidating collective capacities to counter common challenges, certain aspects such as **coastal and offshore security** have also been given equal impetus. The Indian Navy's strategy for 'Coastal and Offshore Security' describes the ways by which cooperative framework and coordination mechanisms will be strengthened and developed. The Navy executes this role in close coordination with the Indian Coast Guard, central ministries and agencies, state governments, port authorities and several other stakeholders.

We have set-up a chain of coastal radar stations, of which 46 stations are up and running. Eighty-seven Automatic Identification System stations over mainland and island territories have also been set-up. All these have been made operational and integrated. We have also set-up a **National Command Control Communication and Information (or NC3I) Network,** integrating 51 stations of the Navy and the Coast Guard. These initiatives enable us to progressively increase Maritime Domain Awareness in our primary areas of maritime interest.

The Indian Navy is also assisting partner-states by setting-up **Coastal Radar Surveillance Systems** and mutual sharing of shipping information through White Shipping Information Exchange agreements. We have already concluded agreements with 21 countries and one multinational construct so far and are in the process of expanding it further. The availability of a consolidated picture to all users as a result of this agreement significantly enhances the strategic Maritime Domain Awareness in the region.

As you may be aware, we commissioned an Information Fusion Centre (IFC-IOR) last year to further our commitment towards achieving collective maritime security in the IOR. The **IFC--IOR is a collaborative construct;** to enhance maritime security and safety. We also aim to work closely with multinational constructs and information fusion centres. Additionally, the IFC-IOR would work towards capability building in the region, coordination of incident response and disaster relief and, in time, also share submarine safety information. We are looking forward to liaison Officers from Friendly Foreign Countries (FFCs) to be a part of this construct.

To further augment regional understanding and sharing of best practices, the Navy recently hosted a Maritime Information Sharing Workshop (MISW) which was attended by over 41 delegates from 29 countries of the IOR and beyond. Various important concepts surrounding maritime terrorism, piracy, human and drug trafficking, humanitarian assistance and disaster relief were discussed and exercised amongst stakeholders.

Moving on, the strategy for **'Maritime Force and Capacity Development'** remains mindful of the long lead time and high investment costs required in naval capacity building. Naval forces need to be versatile and capability-driven, while catering to present and future threats. The future Navy must be able to operate across the entire spectrum of conflict; tackle security contingencies and undertake humanitarian missions equally efficiently when called upon to do so.

This future trajectory would be shaped by our robust capability development programme and remain strongly anchored in **indigenisation** and **Self-Reliance**. The Indian Navy would remain a multi-dimensional force centred on our aircraft carriers with a strong undersea and aviation component. It is a matter of pride that 49 of the 51 warships and submarines under construction are being built in Indian shipyards at the present time.

The Indian Navy has thus emerged as a **'Combat Ready, Credible and Cohesive Force'**, which is keeping pace with the rapid, changes in the environment and is ready to any challenge to protect the maritime interests of our nation.

Having covered our present maritime security strategy, I would now throw some light on the future trajectory of our strategy in the region.

Firstly, the Indian Navy would remain **deployed** in our areas and sectors of maritime interest in the IOR.

Secondly, our vision for the region would be strongly seeded in **collaborative partnerships** with like-minded states. We would continue to engage with our partners to enhance interoperability, which would be fundamental in addressing common security challenges of the region.

Thirdly, we would remain committed towards enhancing the security quotient of the region, maintaining our role as the **Net Security Provider** in our extended maritime neighbourhood.

Overall, I assure you that the Indian Navy is maintaining a close watch on the evolving security dynamics and their implications on the maritime security of India. We are well poised not only to meet our maritime security challenges, but are also ready to take on the larger role of contributing to the security of the region.

Some Thoughts for Students

I use this opportunity to speak to the future leaders of India sitting in this hall...the students. Having spoken about the challenges that we face in the maritime domain and our approach to counter them, let me now share a few thoughts that are close to my heart.

First of all... Who is a student? One, who 'seeks' to learn, is a student. Being a student is not a status in life but a state of mind. It is an 'attitude', which one has towards everything in life. Therefore, you have to realise that learning is a continuous process and not restricted to the classroom. Either you are a student for life or you are not a student at all. However, it is natural that you will cross the threshold of this college one day. Thus, the next question that should confront you is, where do you go from here?

The answer to this question is never a simple or straight one. Some people will tell you to safely follow the beaten path, while others will ask you to take risks and follow your dreams. Some will tell you that a bright future lies abroad and others will ask you to seek your fortunes within the country. I can only assure you that in a short while from now, you will have countless options in front of you! I want you to remember that we are defined by the choices we make and undoubtedly the choice of pursuing a profession is an important one. Therefore, I will try and help streamline your thoughts.

It is my belief that your profession is not a measure of success in life. What decides your value is the **extent of your excellence** in that profession. Just as an example, I would like you to look at the list of alumni of your University. There are artists, civil servants, diplomats, judges, lawyers, media professionals, sportspersons, politicians, writers, bankers, actors, soldiers—the list just goes on. Their diversity of vocations and the magnitude of success vindicate what I just said.

Whatever profession you finally decide to choose, remember to love and respect your country. We are fortunate to be born and living in India and we must always remember the sacrifices and contributions of our countrymen; you must, therefore, always judge all your actions by asking, 'How will my action benefit my country?'

I would also like you to remember that **"Tough times don't last but tough people do".** Successful people use their experience of facing and overcoming adversity as their source of strength.

I would emphasise here, that if you want to be successful, you will have to learn to take both success and failure in your stride. This very important lesson of life is best summed-up by our former President, Shri A.P.J. Abdul Kalam when he famously remarked and I quote, "If you fail, never give up because FAIL is an acronym for ***First Attempt in Learning".***

I, sincerely wish that your choice of higher education and profession will be governed by your fiery passion as well as sharp intelligence, which will also help you make the best use of your aptitude. Here, I would like you to remember that once you have set your heart on something, work hard with sincerity and dedication.

Importance of being a good human being. But while you get occupied in the mesh of your professional pursuits, I would invite your attention to the importance of being good. In this regard, you can follow Mother Teresa's famous saying and I quote, "A life not lived for others is not a life". By this I mean, that, in your quest to get ahead in the game of life, please remember that each one of us has a role to play in the advancement of our society. Just as many people played an important role in shaping your lives, you also have a duty to do your bit as you move along. I would also urge each one of you to imbibe 'kindness' as one of your inherent personality traits. Only if you are kind to others around you, will you be able to empathise with them.

Conclusion

Ladies and gentlemen, before I conclude, I would like to once again reiterate that in a world where maritime issues are taking centre stage, I am very happy that many organisations and the audience such as you are contributing regularly towards maritime awareness in the country. I would recommend you to engage in discussions and debates that cover the entire spectrum of issues having a bearing on the nation's maritime security.

I would further urge you all in the interest of the future of our country, to inculcate maritime thinking and comprehend the need for sea power for the nation.

Thank you, *Jai Hind and Shano Varuna*!

2

India's Challenges in the Current Geo-Strategic Construct

Gen. Bipin Rawat,
UYSM, AVSM, SM, VSM, COAS,
Chief of the Army Staff

Introduction

Let me begin with a brief overview of **National Security** issues, so that the current security canvas can be visualized in the right perspective.

India's Strategic Vision is in harmony with our traditional character as a peaceful and responsible nation. We have always played a constructive role in international relations.

Our **Security Policy** flows from two cardinals, i.e., we have no extra-territorial ambitions and no desire to transplant our ideology on others.

India's **National Security Aim** aligns to our need to 'ensure a conductive internal and external environment for unhindered economic progress and social-political development; for enabling India to assume its rightful role in the emerging world order'.

The National Security Aim translates into our **National Security Objectives**. These entail ensuring territorial integrity and creation of a secure internal security environment to mitigate the threats to our unity, to our core values and to the nation's peaceful development. Therefore, India needs to possess an effective capability to prevent destabilization of its immediate neighbourhood and address security concerns of the extended neighbourhood, when required to do so.

As a responsible nuclear state, we follow a policy of no first-use, non-use against non-nuclear states, maintain a posture of minimum credible deterrence and unilateral moratorium of further tests.

The security perspective of a nation, like its partners and competitors, does not remain constant. India is not a member of any military alliance or strategic grouping. Therefore, it needs to maintain the required military capabilities to secure and pursue its National Interests.

Security Deficits

Our tumultuous years of pre-independence have created immense security deficits that need to be addressed on priority. These include historical, economic, security and energy deficits.

Security Environment

Let me now articulate the global and regional security perspectives, which affect us.

Global Security Perspective

(a) The global security environment is evolving rapidly and is now increasingly complex. Trans-national **terrorism** and **radicalism remain at centre stage**. These have bred numerous **hybrid conflicts and greater asymmetric threats** from **non-state actors.**

(b) Asia is emerging as the global centre of gravity. This is due to its fastest growing economies, the biggest producers and consumers of energy, the highest number of nuclear weapon states and those with the highest defence spending. Hence, it is natural for India to play a greater role in regional and international affairs. There are many aspects that lend credence to this. These are the attributes of the gift of geography, the strengths of our culture, presence of natural resources, potential of our population resource, the size of the growing economy, our space capabilities, etc., to name just a few.

(c) China's increased assertiveness in the political, economic and military domains is being witnessed in many regions of the world.

(d) **Territorial disputes**, including over the maritime domain, have sharpened differences between states. These could lead to militaristic approaches and challenges to norms of international law and standards of international behaviour.

(e) Freedom of navigation is essential for unimpeded commerce that fulfils the needs of economic interdependence between nations. Economy, as a driver of geo-politics, will continue to retain its primacy.

(f) **Geo-politics** and **geo-economics** are being affected by a degree of uncertainty of policies and approaches of major powers. Global ramifications of this are yet to be fully discerned.

(g) Certain regions are witnessing rising aspirations. This, in conjunction with weak economic growth and a variety of environment and social crises, are placing **burdens** on **state structures** of a few nations. Such **manifestations** in **our neighbourhood** will have **security implications** for us.

Regional Security Environment

(a) Onthe regional security canvas, **terrorism** and **sectarian conflicts** are an increasing threat to stability. The **Af-Pak region** remains volatile. **Afghanistan** is and shall remain an area of strategic importance to us. We remain committed to capacity building and capability development of the Afghan Defence Forces.

(b) In our neighbourhood, there is a growing recognition of the need to take a united view against cross-border terrorism. This is a positive development. Of course, Pakistan is not one of the countries sharing this perspective.

(c) **China** continues to enhance its influence in the region. It is doing so by increased defence/economic partnerships in the neighbourhood, especially in Pakistan, Maldives, Sri Lanka, and Myanmar. The **China-Pakistan Economic Corridor** passing through Pakistan-Occupied Kashmir challenges India's sovereignty.

India's Security Dilemmas

Before I speak about the current and specific issues, it is important to visualize that we face certain inherent dilemmas that are unique. These are, to an extent, a legacy of our history. Four significant deficits figure here.

(a) Firstly, it is the **colonial legacy** and the **Partition**. These have handed down the Kashmir dispute and the problems of boundary delineation on both the western and northern fronts.

(b) Secondly, as a **developing country** with a **massive population**, we have a serious economic deficit. The bulk of our limited resources go into the much-needed socio-economic development. This leaves very limited resources for security

(c) Thirdly are the security imperatives, which are complex. Apart from the **external security** problems that we are dealing with, there is a variety of internal security issues.

(d) Lastly, there is the **energy deficit.** While our economy grows at an impressive rate, it also increases our dependence on imports. At the grand strategic level, this has obvious repercussions.

Let me now speak about certain specific issues.

China

Firstly, speaking about China:

(a) Pockets of **dispute** and **contested claims** to territory continue to exist. These are due to differing perceptions on the alignment of the Line of Actual Control (LAC). **Transgressions** across the Line of Actual Control do happen. We do however have joint mechanisms in place to address such situations.

(b) The **Chinese armed forces** have made significant progress in capabilities for force mobilisation, application and sustenance of operations. This is due to the development of infrastructure of military significance. Their force reorganisation along with developing capabilities in space and network-centric warfare is likely to provide them greater synergy in force application.

(c) The **recent standoff** is a consequence of the Chinese attempting to change the status quo.

(d) We continue to engage with China at the political, economic and military levels and **confidence-building measures** are in place.

Pakistan

(a) Pakistan continues to wage a **proxy war** in Jammu and Kashmir. This inimical design entails employing non-state actors. Attempts are being made to expand infiltration attempts across the borders in other states as well along India's western frontiers.

(b) The increasing presence of transnational actors in Pakistan with fundamentalist ideologies is a matter of concern. Pakistan's unabated reliance and support to Jihadi groups has serious ramifications. This can lead to the possibility of Pakistan being a conduit for the eastward spread of the fundamentalist and IS ideology. This lends a complex dimension to the threat not only for us, but also for other countries of South and East Asia, including China.

(c) The Indian Army remains committed in operations that are highly demanding in terms of skills and endurance to counter Pakistan's designs. **Cease-fire violations** on the Line of Control, attempts to aid **infiltration** by Pakistan army posts and trans LoC actions, are being and will continue to be responded to proactively. We shall take all the action necessary to negate, mitigate and destroy elements involved in planning or taking action inimical to India's security interests. Punitive response options will be in a time, place and manner of own choosing.

Internal Security and other Threats

Let me now speak about the internal security and other threats that confront us.

(a) Proxy War

(i) The proxy war being waged from across the border is likely to continue in the near future. Terrorists and their handlers are constantly innovating tactics to throw up new challenges for the security forces. These entail engineering mass protests across major populated centres, triggering rural unrest to impede ongoing security forces operations and the making of false accusations.

(ii) **Domination** and **Intelligence-based operations** by the Indian Army are on. I wish to make a special mention of the Jammu & Kashmir Police and the Central Armed Police Forces. They have supported our operations and displayed immense commitment and resilience.

We shall continue to work with all stakeholders towards addressing the situation.

(b) Insurgency in the North East

The security situation in the insurgency-affected areas of the North-east remains stable and under control. However, enduring solutions remain a challenge due to diverse demands of ethnic groups and various militant outfits. Few insurgent groups, non-aligned and non-committal to the peace process, are attempting to keep the region restive. They are doing so by exploiting ethnic, tribal and communal fissures. These notwithstanding, units of the Indian Army and Assam Rifles deployed there are doing a commendable job.

(c) Left Wing Extremism

Violence levels in the Left Wing Extremism affected areas over the years have declined. However, the threat from Maoist cadres continues to simmer. We are witness to the periodic incidents of attacks on security forces. The Indian Army, by virtue of its core competencies, shall continue to support the Central Armed Police Forces and State Police Forces in a **'Training and Advisory'** role.

(d) Hybrid Threats and Non-traditional Challenges

As a nation, we continue to face some hybrid and non-traditional challenges too.

(i) Growing threats to critical national infrastructure, national grids and networks from **cyber** and outer **space** are transcending the political and geographical divide. The rising instability in our neighbourhood has increased the probability of the proliferation of **weapons of mass destruction** in the hands of non-state actors. **Drug trafficking, illegal migration, fake currency, human trafficking,** socio-economic **disparity** and widespread demographic, **religious** and **linguistic divides**, remain significant challenges.

(ii) **Climate change** has manifested in disruptive seasonal patterns with increased incidents of natural disasters. Rising water levels in coastal areas could trigger cross-border mass migration of people. Competition for natural resources, including water, would be further exacerbated with climate change. Since these changes affect the land where people live, our Land Forces would remain at the forefront of national response strategy.

Current Endeavours and Focus Areas

The issues that I have spoken thus far, bring out the security challenges that the nation faces today. To counter these, the Indian Army, as the largest component of the Armed Forces, plays a pivotal role. So, let me now speak about certain **Indian Army-specific issues** that are **pertinent** for **addressing national security imperatives.**

Firstly, I shall bring out some of our ongoing **endeavours** and **focus areas.**

Capability Development: While capability development is an ongoing process, it needs regular audit, review and resurgence. This is necessary to keep it congruent to the extant security imperatives. We do have some force asymmetries with our adversaries, but these are sector/theatre specific factors. These asymmetries are addressed when the capabilities of all the three Services are augmented for synergistic employment. The army-specific requirements of force modernisation and making up critical deficiencies remain key focus areas. So far, the dependence on imports had made the situation difficult, but, with the 'Make in India' endeavour and thrust on indigenization, we are on the right path to address our capability requirements in a holistic manner. This shall also result in developing our national defence industrial base.

Responder during **Natural Disasters:** In times of disaster, time is the essence. The Armed Forces invariably become de-facto, the first responders due to their pan-India presence, especially in remote areas.

In addition, the Services and the Army **possess key capabilities** that can be employed during these emergencies.

(a) Intrinsic expertise that resides with us is:

(i) **Intelligence, Surveillance, Reconnaissance** and a 24×7×365 functional **communications** infrastructure.

(ii) A network of **field hospitals** and **medical facilities** even in the most far-flung areas.

(iii) Trained **engineers** and **earth-moving equipment** that can facilitate emergency construction and repair of roads and bridges.

(iv) **Transportation assets,** both surface and aerial.

(b) **The precious lives saved by the men in uniform** during some of the recent emergencies are: during the Sikkim Earthquake—971; Uttarakhand floods—38,720; J&K floods—160,129 and Chennai floods—19,600.

(c) In 2016 and 2017, 17 columns of the Indian Army were requisitioned for assistance in law and order situations while 57 columns were deployed for 36 different disaster relief situations.

Response to other Emergencies. Core competencies also exist with us in specialized fields of **Hostage Rescue, Bomb Disposal, Underwater Diving, Search** and **Rescue, Heliborne Insertion** and **Extraction,** etc. We have rendered assistance in such contingencies whenever required.

Capability Development of CAPFs

(a) The Indian Army is proud to share its core expertise, experience and training facilities to augment the capabilities of the Central Armed Police Forces.

(b) We are training Central Armed Police personnel in Counter-terrorism operations. Selected CAPF and State Police battalions undergo pre-induction training prior to deployment in disturbed areas.

It also entails counter-improvised explosive device training and attachment of CAPF personnel with infantry battalions.

International Engagements. The Indian Army contributes significantly to defence diplomacy initiatives. These entail visits, training, joint exercises and defence industry-related exchange programs.

(a) Our **joint exercises** with international partners have evolved, in both conduct and content. Our engagements in 2017 are with Australia, China, France, Kazakhstan, Malaysia, Thailand, Russia, the UK and the USA.

(b) To exploit our expertise and training infrastructure, almost 2,500 vacancies in a large number of courses in our training establishments have been offered to cadets and trainees from friendly foreign countries. Tailor-made courses are being run for trainees from Afghanistan, Bangladesh, Nigeria, Sri Lanka, Turkmenistan and Tajikistan.

(c) We have **10 training teams** deployed overseas. These initiatives are important building blocks for enduring partnerships with friendly nations.

UN Commitments: Despite our operational and internal security commitments, the Indian Army has been ensuring contribution to United Nations peacekeeping missions. Presently, Indian Army personnel are deployed in nine missions. The fragile security situation and operating environment in most of these mission areas is very challenging. Despite that, our officers and men have been giving a fine account of themselves. This has been acknowledged by the UN, repeatedly. The contribution and sacrifices of the Indian Armed Forces adds significance to India's stance on the need for UN Security Council reforms.

Vision for the Future

Let me now highlight a few key pursuits that are imperative for us from the perspective of the future.

Jointness and Integration: The unique capabilities of each Service can be best exploited when they fight as an integrated whole. Joint employment of capabilities is a force multiplier. These will sustain true **Effect-Based Operations (EBO)** through **networking of assets**. Domains that are feasible for joint capability augmentation are **Space**-based applications, **Air support, Air Defence, Intelligence, Communications, Electronic Warfare, Information Warfare, Logistics, Training, Joint Staff** functioning and **Rear Area Security**. The three Services are jointly engaging in pursuits to explicitly define an approach to deal with future imperatives.

Sustaining Training Benchmarks: The technological progression, dynamic security environment and demands of an envisaged future battlefield portend a challenge. These demand a continuous quest to sustain the required training benchmarks. We are engaged in a pursuit to envision the various sub-systems that make up the whole system of 'Preparedness'. They entail equipment serviceability, proficiency of each man on his designated equipment, building in redundancy and exercising the 'man-equipment pair'. These are being done under simulated battlefield conditions; these requirements need to be sustained to cater for new technologies and turnover of manpower. The bottom line is to put in motion a unique action plan to ensure that training standards are sustained above the designated benchmarks.

Expanding Strategic Horizons: As the nation envisions its future aspirations, towards seeking its rightful place in the global and regional power structure, the need to protect its security interests will increase. The implications accruing from being a 'net security provider in the region', dictate possession of commensurate capabilities. These requirements mandate engagement with the politico-civil set-up at various levels in the country and with national coordinating agencies of international partners. Awareness of institutions, procedures, executing agencies and scope of such requirements as they unfold is an imperative. It needs to be appreciated that the 'ground zero' situation, where such requirements may come up, will have unique challenges. These may even entail combat response for self-defence or saving precious lives. The Indian Army has the vital 'boots on the ground' to form the crucial component of such tri-Services components.

Adapting to Future Warfare. The nature of warfare has undergone remarkable change. The pace, lethality and intensity powered by the latest technologies require militaries to adapt in order to succeed. The hybrid nature of the battlefield has blurred the distinction between front and rear, friend and foe and combatants and civilians. In the network-centric environment, modern state-of-art weapon systems can easily out match obsolete technology and create force asymmetry. Technological infusion commensurate with contemporary developments shall remain an enduring pursuit.

Conclusion

To conclude my talk, I would like to mention that international politics is about applying national power, within the international system, in support of national and collective interest. The **objectives** being pursued, and the manner of their pursuit, involve the **development, coordination** and **use** of the **instruments of national power**. These are essentially **diplomacy, economic power and military power**. Each of these three instruments has to be used in relation with the others. It will very often be the case that diplomatic means are only successful if they are backed up with an implicit or declared threat to use other means if diplomacy fails. **To be an effective instrument of national security, the military**

cannot operate in isolation. It has to be part of a fully coordinated and coherent grand strategy in which **diplomacy and economics** are equally **important**.

The emerging security environment is full of uncertainties. Within this maze of ambiguity, we need to correctly identify and define our security concerns that affect our national aspirations. I am confident that the Indian Army with its bedrock character built on secular credentials, robust discipline and astute professionalism, shall meet the aspirations of an emergent India.

Jai Hind

3

Transformation of the Indian Air Force: Challenges and Opportunities

Air Chief Marshal Arup Raha,
PVSM, VM, ADC,
Chairman, Chief of the Staff Committee and Chief of the Air Staff

Introduction

I must begin by paying my tribute to General B.C. Joshi, a distinguished soldier who shared a unique and close relationship with the academia. His diverse contributions to encourage research in the field of National Security distinguish him as a visionary ahead of his time. His efforts in furthering University–Armed Forces interaction enabled officers from the Armed Forces to engage in academic research on defence and security-related issues at institutions of higher learning. He was instrumental in establishing the Army Institute of Technology, Pune, for children of Army personnel. The Armed Forces shall forever remain indebted to him for his patronage of higher studies.

Scope

While the primary focus of today's talk will be on *'Transformation of the IAF with regard to the Challenges and Opportunities'* as I perceive them, I shall also touch upon certain relevant aspects of military power in general.

Evolution of Military Power

Traditionally, the military power of a nation was determined by the strength of its army/land forces. Subsequently, the naval and seafaring powers capitalised on the inherent advantages of maritime power and colonised the world. Aerospace power, which is the youngest, only 110 years old, provided immense relief and freedom from surface friction inherent in land and sea operations and brought about a major transformation in the concepts of warfighting.

Recent conflicts have aptly demonstrated the ability of air power to influence the outcome of land and sea operations and that their success has been uniquely dependent on the exploitation of the third dimension. Air power plays a major role in protecting own forces and has the ability to delay enemy mobilisation and degrade the capability and morale of enemy troops through offensive action. Today, air power has matured and has grown out of the shadow of its sister Services. It has proved its mettle in several conflicts and is the sharp edge of combat power. The future will witness the continued pre-eminence of aerospace power as a primary instrument of choice in most operational contingencies, be it war or peace, including HADR operations.

When we trace the history of nations, we find that the Great Powers have demonstrated mastery over the creation, deployment and use of military power to achieve their national objectives. Comprehensive National Power is governed by several factors such as economic and human resource development, scientific and technological advancement, availability of natural resources, etc. In my opinion, military power is perhaps the most important component, second only to economic potential. When we look around, we observe that nations that play an important role in the international arena invest adequately in military power. India is destined to play an important role in ushering peace and stability in the region, if not the world, because of its economic, military, HR and soft power.

The composition of the military power of a nation is governed by three factors. The Threat perception and its mitigation, National objectives and aspirations; and Budget constraints. Threat perception would determine the size of various forces and its composition while budgetary constraints would require prioritisation amongst competing demands.

Our national objectives are well enshrined in the form of declarations in Panchsheel, the Non-Aligned Movement (NAM), active participation in the United Nations, etc. Though we have no territorial ambitions, border disputes with some of our neighbours have resulted in several conflicts in the past.

To avoid conflicts and deter war in the future, we must possess requisite offensive capability. Future conventional wars are likely to be short, swift and intense. To achieve the desired end states and objectives rapidly, there is a requirement to have a national instrument that would be unique with attributes of speed, reach, footprint and precision to fit the bill.

A brief scan of the geo-political and security environment indicates that the strategic gravity of the world has shifted to Asia and the Pacific, which has numerous security challenges. The peaceful rise of nations is essential for peace and stability in the region. Pakistan being a member of the Global War on Terror (GWOT) needs to do more to prevent its soil being used by terrorist groups, especially those operating against India. The rise of the Islamic State in the Middle East has given rise to serious security concerns. We need to be prepared for the entire spectrum of conflicts ranging from sub-conventional and conventional to the non-conventional.

IAF Today

The IAF today, along with the Indian Navy and Indian Army, is poised to contribute in stabilising the region. It has enabled the nation to have a strategic presence. It performs four classical roles as a multi-spectrum strategic force.

Firstly, **Power Projection**. Aircrafts such as Su-30, Flight refuelling aircraft, Airborne warning and control system, C-17, C-130, etc., have enhanced our strategic reach and footprint. Certain capabilities have been aptly demonstrated during the Humanitarian Aid and Disaster Relief (HADR) operations in Yemen and Nepal.

Second is **Credible Deterrence**. A credible IAF with appropriate force levels and precision weapons has been one of the major contributory factors in deterring our adversaries from precipitating a major confrontation since 1971.

Third is **Protection**: What often goes unnoticed is the 24x7 air defence provided by the IAF to protect the sovereignty of the nation's airspace frontiers. With 6,000 civil and 1,500 military flights daily, radars keep churning and fighter aircraft and helicopters are kept ready for action, if required. However, the biggest challenge that shall remain is the mitigation of unregulated sub-con aerial threats as well as an exponential increase in civil aviation.

Fourth **classical role is Peace Time tasks**. Air maintenance in the Northern as well as North-Eastern sectors is the lifeline of the ground forces and the IAF lifts close to 35,000 tonnes annually by fixed and rotary wing aircraft.

Logistics support to para military forces engaged in controlling left-wing extremism is another major peacetime task being performed by the IAF. Since 2009, the IAF has flown a substantial number of sorties to airlift a large number of personnel and logistics supplies.

In recent times, the IAF's performance in HADR operations has been exceptional. Its contributions in rescue and relief operations during flash floods in Leh in 2010, floods in Uttarakhand in 2013 and in J&K in 2014 have been outstanding. During the operations in Yemen, 2,100 Indians and other nationals were evacuated at short notice from a distant location in a co-ordinated operation with other agencies.

In the recently conducted 'Op Maitri' in the aftermath of the Nepal earthquake, the IAF won accolades from the international community for its swift and overwhelming response. The time from notification to take-off was less than two hours. Over 1,700 sorties were flown for the rescue and transportation of 12,000 people to safer areas and to airlift 1,350 tonnes of relief material.

These operations have resulted in a perception change towards the image of our nation as a whole. The leadership role for India in HADR has been acknowledged worldwide and this has come about through sustained performance and pro-active action.

Challenges

In addition to threats from unregulated sub-conventional aerial vehicles mentioned earlier, there are certain unique challenges faced by the IAF.

(a) **Terrain and Weather**. The IAF operates over some of the most diverse terrain and climatic conditions, ranging from snow-clad mountain ranges, riverine, northern plains, tropical forests, the Thar Desert, peninsular coastal areas, vast oceans and island territories. The highest Advanced Landing Ground (ALG) for fixed-wing aircraft in the world, Daulat Beg Oldie, and helipads in Siachen often require aircraft to operate at the limit of their flight envelope with minimal margin for error. It requires exceptional skills, professionalism and guts to fly in such challenging conditions.

(b) **Targeting**. Engaging targets in mountainous terrain calls for special skills. Static targets in deserts are difficult to identify and special sensors are required to detect targets through foliage in jungles. This calls for specially-trained crew and state-of-the-art sensors.

(c) **Maintenance**. Sand, dust, heat and humidity are major challenges in Indian terrain and climatic conditions. Operating in desert terrain requires special attention and care for sensitive avionics. Operating in humid or coastal areas offers its own challenge in terms of corrosion of metallic parts.

(d) **Exploitation of Technology**. The IAF operates a mixed inventory with diverse origins such as European, Russian, US and Indian. Inter-operability and dynamic inventory management are major challenges. Standardisation of different operational and maintenance philosophies is a challenge in itself.

(e) **Lack of Indigenous Capabilities**. Lack of indigenous capabilities leads to over dependence on foreign original equipment manufacturers (OEM). This in turn affects product support, the repair and overhaul (ROH) of airframes and engines and turn-around-time (TAT) of aggregates.

(f) **Budget Constraints**. Budget constraints will continue to affect the IAF like any other Air Force. Therefore, it is important to prioritise our capital acquisitions and at the same time have adequate revenue support to meet the running costs for optimum exploitation of our assets. The exchange rate variation (ERV), inflation and escalating fuel costs must be borne in mind during various stages of planning.

(g) **Acquisition Process**. The acquisition process as laid out in the DPP takes a long time to fructify. Since military procurements are often governed by the overall national security strategy, government-to-government deals provide a more comprehensive and faster means.

Opportunities

(a) The exponential growth of the civil aviation and space sectors, both with potential for dual use, has given rise to numerous opportunities for the growth of the aerospace power of our country.

(b) Enhanced thrust on indigenisation, transfer of technology and added impetus on 'Make in India' policy will redefine the aviation eco-system and result in enhanced private sector participation.

(c) Military industrial complexes which produce most military hardware in Western Europe, Russia and the USA are crucial to the economy of these countries. Peace and stability in the developed world including the USA has resulted in the downsizing of forces and a consequent fall in demand for military hardware. On the other hand, demands in Asia are increasing. India and China will be major customers who will sustain the sales and performance of these complexes in the coming years. We must capitalise on these dynamics to build upon our indigenous aviation industry.

Transformation Plan

The IAF is evolving into a multi-spectrum strategic force. To achieve the goals laid out in its Long-term Integrated Perspective Plan (LTIPP) 2027, the IAF is following a three-pronged approach.

(a) **Preserve and Maintain.** Preserve and maintain its legacy fleets and equipment to sustain operational capability.

(b) **Upgrade and Improve.** Carry out life extension and mid-life upgrade inducting new technology and weapons to keep them operationally relevant.

(c) **Replace/Enhance.** Replace obsolete assets with new acquisitions such as Light Combat Aircraft (LCA), Medium Multi-role Combat Aircraft (MMRCA), Advanced Medium Combat Aircraft (AMCA), etc. Towards this end, operationalisation of C-130J and C-17 has led the way by enhancing IAF's strategic airlift capability. Similarly, operationalisation of MI-17 V5 has greatly enhanced the tactical airlift capability of the IAF. Induction of Chinooks and Apache will be the way forward.

Focus areas based on transformation plan will involve:

(a) Induction of new weapon platforms such as fifth-generation fighter aircraft, MMRCA, force enhancers like Multi-role tanker transport/AWACS/Airborne early warning and Control aircraft, Surface-to-air guided weapons, Radars, etc.

(b) Increase potency of existing equipment through enhanced electronic warfare (EW) capability, better weapons and increased serviceability of weapon platforms.

(c) Build Op infrastructure such as weapon and aircraft storage areas, labs, as well as upgrading operating surfaces.

(d) Optimise training pattern suited to the assets available and enmeshing virtual training system for fine-tuning of the training pattern of personnel to absorb state-of-the-art technology and new inductions.

(e) Focus on quality of life and standard of living to meet the aspirations of air-warriors in terms of good accommodation, sports and medical infrastructure and education facilities for children.

(f) International co-operation through bilateral and multi-lateral exercises to enhance inter-operability and learn and adopt the best practices from other air forces.

(g) Network-centric warfare will remain a focus area and involves integrating ground, air and space-based networks.

(h) Warfare in future would be extensively fought in space and cyberspace and the IAF must be prepared to deal with new forms of silent warfare.

Conclusion

Over the last hour, I have provided a brief overview of roles of the IAF and its tasks, challenges, opportunities, transformation plans and focus areas. Any operational contingency in the future will demand control of the air, situational awareness & ISR, using aerospace assets and precision strike capability. With its vision and acquisitions, the IAF, over the years, has been transforming itself into a multi-spectrum strategic force with an increased strategic footprint. Its capability in terms of air mobility, heavy lift, NCW, cyber and space domains have continued to grow. The relevance of aerospace power in future threats to the environment cannot be over emphasised.

The IAF's core competency in exploitation of aerospace power, especially its offensive capability, is an effective deterrence against a conflict being precipitated. Aerospace power will thus remain the prime instrument of military power.

Capability building is a continuous and long term endeavour. It requires visionary planning, committing national resources and a synergistic approach of all stakeholders.

Jai Hind

4

Indian Navy: Maritime Power for National Prosperity

Admiral D.K. Joshi,
PVSM, AVSM, YSM, NM, VSM
Chief of the Naval Staff

It is a privilege to be here today to deliver this year's General B.C. Joshi Memorial Lecture. The Late General was not only a distinguished soldier but also had a unique and close relationship with the academia, particularly with Pune University. He was instrumental in setting up the Chattrapati Shivaji Chair in Policy Studies at this University, as also a Resident Scholars Programme with the aim of enabling officers from the Armed Forces to engage in academic research on national security affairs at institutions of higher learning. Today, nearly two decades after his untimely demise, the General is fondly remembered as a 'scholar warrior' who raised the bar of intellectual soldiering in independent India. It was only in the fitness of things that he was honoured with a Doctor of Science degree by the Kumaon University in 1994, at a time when he had achieved an iconic image not only in his native (Uttarakhand) state but in the whole country. With this tradition of intellectualism, it is not surprising that the credit for introducing a humane operational culture in the Army goes to Gen. Joshi. His 'Ten Commandments', issued as an 'aide memoire' to troops serving in disturbed areas, exemplify that ethos. Indeed, his diverse contributions to encourage research in the field of national security and his involvement in environment protection distinguish him as a visionary ahead of his time.

The theme for my talk today has been chosen for two reasons. Firstly, it is inspired by a pertinent point made by Gen. Joshi during his address to the All India Vice-Chancellor's Conference at this very University in November 1994, barely five days before he passed away. He had questioned those who looked at defence and development in conflicting economic terms. The key point that the General made then was that defence and development go hand in hand and there is no separating the two. Taking a lead from there and applying it to today's environment, I thought it would be apt to expand on the theme **'Indian Navy—Maritime Power for National Prosperity'** to highlight the key contributions of our Navy to the nation's march towards progress and prosperity. The second reason is that it also happened to be the theme for our Navy Week.

Ladies and gentlemen, we, in the Navy, believe that development and national security are but two sides of the same coin. The only reasonable conclusion that emerges from the old 'guns versus butter' argument is that the choice between development and security cannot be a zero-sum game. The past sixty-six years of our independent existence have shown that a secure environment is an essential pre-requisite for the unhindered economic growth for any nation. A secure environment is ensured only when a nation demonstrates the capability of preserving and furthering its national interests, wherever they may exist, and the willingness to act decisively in their protection when the situation so demands.

Concepts of **'National Security'** and **'National Power'** have evolved with the dynamics of geo-politics and national priorities. Earlier, security was synonymous with defence of territorial integrity and national power was military-centric. However, with globalization and economic integration, ideas such as **'Comprehensive Security'** and **'Comprehensive National Strength'** have gained currency. For any nation, these encompass, beyond military dimensions, economic, societal, energy and environmental security, which are inter-related and centred towards economic prosperity and social development. It is in this context that we see the Navy as a maritime power contributing to the nation's quest for prosperity.

A strong and versatile Navy not only safeguards territory, but also enables the creation of a peaceful periphery to facilitate socio-economic growth. Before I dwell upon the many ways in which the Navy discharges its responsibilities, it is important to situate ourselves in the right historical context to appreciate how the economic fortunes of our nation have been intrinsically and intricately linked to the sea. A peek into our maritime past would aid comprehension of the pervasive linkage between maritime power and economic destiny.

Let me begin my recall of the past with the famous statement that our first Prime Minister, Pandit Jawaharlal Nehru, made in March 1958, at the reception ceremony of INS *Mysore*, the second cruiser to be acquired by the then fledgling Indian Navy. I quote: "*...from this ship I look at India and think of our country and its geographic situation—on three sides there is the sea and on the fourth high mountains—in a sense our country maybe said to be in the very lap of an ocean. In these circumstances, I ponder over our close links with the sea and how the sea has brought us together. From time immemorial, the people of India have had very intimate connections with the sea. They had trade with other countries and they had also built ships. Later on, the country became weak. Now that we are free, we have once again reiterated the importance of the sea.* ***We cannot afford to be weak at sea ... history has shown that whatever power controls the Indian Ocean has, in the first instance, India's seaborne trade at her mercy, and in the second, India's very independence itself.***" No one other than the first Prime Minister could have made the point better in his characteristic eloquence.

We are endowed with a rich and proud maritime heritage, which unfortunately has been largely forgotten except among a minority of intellectuals, historians and social scientists. Ancient Indian literature such as the *Vedas*, Buddhist *Jatakas*, Sanskrit, Pali and Persian literature and even the *Old Testament*, bear testimony to the fact that as far back as the Indus Valley civilisation, there was considerable maritime interaction between India, as it existed then, and countries in Africa, Southern Europe, Western Asia and the Far East.

The prominent rulers of ancient India attached high value to maritime affairs. The war office of Mauryan Emperor Chandragupta had, as one of its six boards, a *Nav Parishad* or the 'Board of Admiralty' which controlled national shipping. The cultural and political expeditions of the Kalingas, Mauryas, Cholas and Sri Vijayas took them to far-flung areas such as Sumatra, Burma, the Malayan Peninsula, Java, Thailand and other countries in Indochina. The effects of this cultural interaction are evident there even today. During a diplomatic assignment in Singapore in the late 1990s, I got to observe firsthand the tell-tale signs of pervasive Indian cultural influence in South-East Asia. Just to give an example, the motto of the Indonesian Navy, 'Jalesveva Jayamahe', is in Sanskrit and means 'Victorious on the Sea'. Likewise, the Indonesian Air Force and Army have also adopted mottos from Sanskrit. There are numerous other examples. Anyone who has visited Bangkok would know that the airport is named Suvarnabhoomi or the 'Land of Gold'. The Borobudur temple in Java and the Angkor Vat temple in Cambodia are monumental testimonies of Indian religious and architectural influences dating back to the 9th and 12th centuries, respectively. The seas acted as the medium of this cultural permeation.

I am emphasising these facts because most of our citizens, much less foreigners, remain ignorant of their inherited rich maritime heritage, and the judicious use of the seas by their ancient forebears for economic, political and cultural purposes. Unfortunately, during the medieval era, the Indian Ocean also facilitated the economic and political subjugation of the sub-continent by colonial powers. During this period, apart from a few intrepid sailors such as Kanhoji Angre, the great Maratha admiral, and Kunjali Marakkars of Calicut, most continental rulers of India displayed a rueful 'sea blindness' that ultimately led to their downfall. Today we must consider ourselves fortunate to be living in an era where the country is witnessing a maritime ascendency after a substantially long period of indifference to this economically and politically significant domain.

Having situated ourselves in the appropriate context, allow me also to define the linkage between security and economic prosperity.

As enunciated earlier, globalisation has given the term 'security' itself a more all-encompassing connotation. **Security** today depends on a **combination of many diverse, yet inter-related factors, centred on economic prosperity and social development.** While economic affordability provides the means for military wherewithal, competing with the requirements of fulfilling the aspirations of people, uplifting masses from poverty, and for transitioning to a knowledge economy, all these impinge upon national security. This defines security's symbiotic relation with socio-economic development, whereas national security provides conducive external and internal environments for socio-economic growth. These developmental activities in turn are building blocks of national security.

Here I would like to briefly touch upon the prevailing security environment and evolving strategic challenges that influence India's socio-economic growth.

In the world around us today, the regional and global power balances are shifting rapidly. The leading economics of the world have suffered most in the global economic slump, which has also accelerated the contrasting and simultaneous rise of several emerging powers. As a result, we have a situation where established and emerging powers are reassessing their relationship, trying to cope with new realities. Globalization has led to varying degrees of inter-dependence between the economies, which in turn are dictating the distribution of power between them. The centre of gravity of the global economy itself is shifting from the West towards Asia. This era of fluid power balances has given considerable room for regional and middle powers for manoeuvring. The impact of the interplay of the geo-strategies of other maritime powers, evolving technologies, economic upheavals and redistribution of military power has become the prime determinant of the strategic outlook of nations. It is in this paradigm that the Navy seeks to provide a secure external environment where the nation's needs of socio-economic growth and prosperity are adequately addressed.

Today, India ranks as the third-largest economy of the world in PPP terms. Our emergence as a nation of global significance has reasserted the linkages of our security and prosperity with maritime environment. Seventy per cent by value, and 90 per cent by volume of our foreign trade is seaborne and the bulk of our energy and resource needs is met through imports via sea routes. Stability in the maritime environment and the safety of associated international shipping lanes is a prime area of attention for a Navy.

To create a secure and conducive external maritime periphery, the Navy has been a catalyst for peace and stability in the Indian Ocean Region. The Navy has been exploiting the wide spectrum of attributes of maritime power to safeguard India's national interests and serve national objectives. The prime attributes, which lend a unique and unrivalled advantage to maritime forces, are mobility, sustenance, reach, flexibility and ability to influence events ashore from the sea.

The Navy has prioritised four traditional, yet vital, roles for itself, namely, **Military, Diplomatic, Constabulary** and **Benign.** The military role of course is the primary and the *raison d'être* of our existence. The use of naval combat power would become necessary in case of an armed external aggression or the need for dissuasive and coercive actions to safeguard our maritime interests. Prominent examples of the Indian Navy's operations in this role are the Junagadh Operations of 1947, the liberation of Goa operations in December 1961, the Indo-Pak War of 1971, Operation *Pawan* in Sri Lanka between 1987-1990, offensive posturing during the Kargil conflict in 1999 and Operation *Parakram* of 2001-2002. Even in the so-called 'peacetime', naval platforms are routinely deployed in all three dimensions for deterrence and to ensure security of the seas around us.

Economic activities and investments tend to avoid areas of turbulence and risk. Consequently, in order to sustain our socio-economic activities, the Navy is driven to ensure stability in India's maritime neighbourhood. Our strategic location and the Navy's status as a leading maritime force in these waters, makes us a responsible actor in the region—a net security provider. This is in complete harmony with our national vision, as recently articulated by the Hon'ble Prime Minister during the foundation-laying ceremony for the Indian National Defence University, when he said: *"We have also sought to assume our responsibility for stability in the Indian Ocean Region. We are well positioned, therefore, to become a net provider of security in our immediate region and beyond."*

On a regular basis, our ships undertake EEZ surveillance and anti-piracy patrols in the waters of friendly nations such as Maldives, Seychelles and Mauritius, on their request. **Naval diplomacy** can also be effective in the form of assistance to foreign countries in times of political crisis or natural calamities. You would recollect the stellar role played by the Navy in Operation *Cactus*, when a coup d'état attempt in Maldives was defeated by us. The prompt humanitarian assistance rendered by our ships in the aftermath of the tsunami of 2004 to affected neighbours such as Sri Lanka, Indonesia and Maldives is another example of our contribution to regional security aligned with the country's foreign policy to create a favourable periphery for social-economic activities.

Our country is blessed with a long coastline which is nearly half the length of our land borders. Our 1,200 islands and resultant Exclusive Economic Zone, which measures almost 2.1 million sq. km., provide us with a treasure of marine wealth and resources. The Navy plays a vital role in ensuring the security of these resources, particularly the strategic vital offshore oil and gas infrastructure, which has been expanding over the years. This role is likely to be accentuated in the future when our nation begins to harness its exclusive rights over deep-sea mining in the Indian Ocean.

Vital amongst our economic interests in the maritime domain is the unimpeded flow of energy. At present, more than 80 per cent of our petroleum consumption is met through sea-borne imports, a figure which continues to rise. Also, considering our limited hydrocarbon reserves and a burgeoning demand, acquiring overseas 'Equity Oil and Gas Assets' has been a vital facet of the nation's strategy for energy security. Indian public and private enterprises have acquired offshore and onshore energy resources across the globe, from Russia to Brazil. Protection of these far-flung assets and their security are essential elements of our national security calculus, the onus of which is primarily on the Navy.

Our operations in the **Constabulary Role** also imply law enforcement and preventive activities to preserve good order at sea. For the last five years, 36 of our warships have been engaged in **anti-piracy operations** in the Northern Indian Ocean, to protect shipping, Indian or otherwise, from Somali pirates. These pirates have attracted global attention after multiple incidents of attacks on ships, followed by hijacking and ransom demands. Our robust actions, such as sinking of four pirate mother ships in 2011, clearly signals India's resolve to curb this menace and have deterred piracy close to the Indian coast. In the Gulf of Aden, no ship under our escort has been pirated during the last four–and-a-half years. Over 2,500 ships have been escorted by the Navy, 40 piracy attempts foiled and more than 120 pirates arrested.

The criticality of naval counter-piracy efforts in the Northern Indian Ocean becomes apparent when we appreciate that over 40,000 vessels transit the high-risk area, many of them destined to Indian ports. The goods carried by them are subjected to war risk as well as kidnap-and-ransom premium by marine insurance companies, in turn raising freight costs. Globally, this additional premium burden due to piracy is estimated to be to the tune of 635 million dollars.

Human security holds special relevance in the maritime domain. More than half of humanity lives within 200 km of the coast, which accounts for only 10 per cent of the available landmass. Tasks such as humanitarian assistance, non-combatant evacuation, disaster relief, search and rescue, medical aid, ordnance disposal, diving assistance, salvage operations, etc., are all under the ambit of the Navy's **Benign Role.** Apart from routinely supporting the Coast Guard in response to distress calls from mariners and fishermen at sea, the Navy has also contributed substantially to flood, earthquake or cyclone relief operations in different parts of the country. Recently, our diving teams were deployed in support of the flood relief and rescue operations in Uttarakhand.

We have the second largest **Diaspora** in the world with an estimated 21 million Indians settled or temporarily working in every major region of the globe. Besides directly contributing to India's economy through remittances, they are also ambassadors of Indian culture and conduits of soft power overseas. The safety and well-being of these Indians is also of concern to us. Aggravation of security conditions due to conflict or calamity may necessitate large-scale homeward movement of this population. Evacuation of our nationals from Lebanon in 2006 and Libya in 2011 are examples of such migration, wherein the Navy played a key role.

The coastline characterized by industry, SEZs, ports and other economic activities is the lifeline of the socio-economic development of India, but is under constant threat of a wide array of non-conventional challenges. After infiltration by terrorists from the sea leading to the 26/11 attacks on Mumbai, the coastal security set-up in the country was revamped to bring about closer coordination between various stakeholders. In accordance with government directives, the Navy has assumed a leadership role in coordinating coastal security in conjunction with Coast Guard, central ministries and agencies, state governments, port authorities and local fishermen.

Let me now invite your attention to an important area where, over the years, we have made key contributions to national developments, capacity building and strengthening of the industrial base. The Indian Navy is committed to supporting indigenization, as a matter of policy, by providing a long-term and firm commitment. We were an early proponent of indigenisation and had reposed faith in Indian shipyards way back in 1961 when INS *Ajay* became the first to be indigenously constructed by M/s GRSE Ltd, Kolkata. Since then, we have not looked back. Today we have acquired a level of confidence with which our first 40,000-ton indigenous aircraft carrier (IAC) is under construction at Cochin Shipyard Limited, and will be launched next week. We are proud of the fact that 46 of the 47 ships and submarines currently on order for the Indian Navy are being constructed in India in both, public as well as private shipyards. Truly, we have transitioned from a "Buyers' Navy, to a Builders' Navy", thus providing a huge fillip to the capabilities of our shipyards and also providing a boost to manufacturing by small and medium enterprises, that function as feeder units to the shipbuilding industry.

"Indian Navy: Maritime Security Through Self-Reliance", our theme for this year's Navy Week, encapsulates our commitment to indignation in quest of strategic autonomy, an imperative for any national power of relevance. Very few select countries globally construct their own ships, aircraft carriers and submarines, including nuclear ones, which is a matter of national pride.

The Navy has also been a staunch supporter of the R&D efforts of the nation's science and technological base. Some of the widely acclaimed projects of the DRDO such as the indigenous sonar program and other strategic technologies have been naval projects. In fact, the Indian Navy enjoys a unique distinction among the three Services of having three DRDO laboratories dedicated to naval research. The Navy has also contributed to our research activities in the Antarctica programme, which dates back to 1981.

The National Hydrographic Office of the Navy has a fleet of oceangoing survey ships and new catamaran hull survey vessels, equipped with state-of-the-art equipment. The department renders yeoman service to the nation through its hydrographic surveys, publication of papers and electronic nautical charts and information, essential for safe navigation. The hydrographic survey of India's coastal waters has facilitated coastal regions. The Indian ports sector is slated for an ambitious perspective growth over this decade. It goes without saying that hydrographic surveys will find an increasing salience in the creation of offshore infrastructure, critical to port development.

On the societal front, the Navy contributes to nation building through the Naval NCC, Sea Cadet Corps and other public outreach activities such as medical camps. We have made dedicated efforts to infuse a spirit of adventure among the young generation by sponsoring sailing, mountaineering and other adventure expeditions. It is worth a mention here that the Naval skiing team is the first Indian team to have successfully undertaken an expedition to both the Poles. In recent times, the record-setting solo circumnavigation voyage of INSV *Mhadei* has attracted the popular attention of the nation.

In summation, let me re-iterate that India's fortunes are overwhelmingly linked to the seas. This reality and the realization that maritime power is vital for safeguarding maritime interests and crucial for national prosperity, will become more and more apparent as we march into the 21st century. The Hon'ble President of India recently reminded us of the indelible linkage between socio-economic prosperity and maritime security and I conclude by quoting him: "*... a nation's social and economic well being is intricately linked to the seas, not only for trade but also how it faces threats to its own security that develop across the seas...our resolve to achieve high growth can be realised only if our maritime frontiers and assets are safe, stable and act as enablers. The Indian Navy, as the primary element of India's maritime power, has the challenging task of safeguarding the country's maritime interests...*"

Ladies and gentlemen, thank you for your kind attention.

Jai Hind

5

Perspective on War in the 21st Century

Lt Gen AK Singh,
PVSM, AVSM, SM, VSM, ADC,
GOC-in-C Southern Command

Introduction

It gives me great pleasure to be with you today, the students and faculty of the Department of Defence and Strategic Studies of Pune University, to deliver this year's General BC Joshi Memorial Lecture. As you know, this endowment aims at promoting informed debate and thought among our wider community of intellectuals on matters affecting national security.

I have chosen to speak to you on "Perspective on War in the 21st Century", as the past couple of decades have seen fundamental and far reaching changes in all spheres of human affairs, driven largely by information technology, which has provided access to influence, resources and thereby the ability to shape events, to myriad groups and individuals something that was the exclusive domain of the state till not very long ago.

As influence grows and stake holders become more numerous and diverse, so the potential for competition, conflict and outright hostilities rises. Indeed the increasing interconnectedness of peoples, economies and cultures is what drives and shapes conflict. Predicting the future is always difficult and risky, but I shall try to do so in context of the trend we can see as the drivers of change in the way state and non-state actors are likely to seek to secure their interests.

A few decades ago, it was relatively easy to talk about the nature of warfare, as it we intimately linked to statecraft, so you indentified an adversary state and prepared yourself accordingly. In fact one could even quantify threats and capabilities to arrive at a predictable outcome. In the 21st century, this is no longer so. Shades of grey have crept in; threats are not easy to quantify and sometimes even to identify. There is a merging, a fusion of various types of warfare; international rules do not apply to adversaries who are not state actors and deterrence, coercion and escalatory dynamics have been turned on the head in a large number of cases.

Against such uncertainty, it is no longer easy to define the capabilities a nation requires to meet its aspirations and obligations and safeguard its vital national interests. To offer perspective against such a background is indeed a daunting task. I therefore intend to cover the subject through a series of questions that need answering before we can arrive at a clear perspective. As a professional soldier, let me try to provide simplified clarity to such complex subject.

To do justice to the subject, I have drawn largely on material from an international seminar on the changing of conflict that I had organised at the Centre for Land Warfare Studies in Delhi in late 2009. I intend to cover the subject in three parts:

(a) **Part I: The Nature of Conflict**

  (i) How is the nature of conflict changing?

  (ii) What are the emerging contours of conflict?

  (iii) Will conventional conflict remain relevant?

  (iv) Are we moving towards hybrid warfare?

(b) **Part II: Strategic Choices.** What strategic choices do nation states have with respect to structuring their armed forces?

(c) **Part III: Adapting to Change**

  (i) How does the changing nature of conflict impact on the role of air and maritime power?

(ii) Is there space for conventional conflict between nuclear states?

(iii) How will the dynamics of deterrence, coercion and escalatory control work against non-state actors?

PART I: THE NATURE OF CONFLICT

The character of warfare is determined more by political, social, economic and strategic imbalances than it is by changes that may occur on the military front. The disintegration of the Soviet Union in 1991 led to the end of the Cold War. However, the cataclysmic airborne terrorist attacks on the US on Sept. 11, 2001 have transformed the definition of security and today we live in an uncertain security scenario of "no war, no peace".

There has been a paradigm shift in the very nature of conflict. Though territorial issues are important, other issues related to historical differences, ideological biases, economic disparity, energy security and water shortage are contributing factors for conflict. Modern day conflicts are not merely confined to states, but have expanded to include sub-nationalities, terrorists, insurgents, religious fanatics and ethnic interests. The nature of conflict today encompasses sabotage, subversion, confrontation and traditional armed conflict. Thus, the state's response needs to be balanced, inclusive and one that incorporates political, economic, societal and military measures.

Various developments in our neighbourhood, particularly in Pakistan and Afghanistan have brought South Asia to the centre stage of sub-conventional conflict and instability. Additionally, terrorism, low intensity conflict motivated by economic disparity, religious fundamentalism, narcotics trade, and the threat of nuclear weapons falling into the wrong hands remain issues of concern in our region. Nations are seeking new ways and means to combat terrorism. In this regard, civil society, human rights organisations, media and law enforcement agencies all have a role to play. In addition, the armed forces must be used optimally to shape an adequate response to such threats.

While there is a sharp decline in direct armed conflict between nations, internal armed conflicts have witnessed an upward trend. The entry of non-state actors has added a new dimension to low intensity conflicts. Responses to such challenges need to be addressed in a focused and credible manner. The conventional armed forces need to maintain an edge by upgrading technologies; intelligence and security agencies need to coordinate nationally and internationally; and cooperative security as a strategy needs to be enforced at regional and international levels.

Future threats will also encompass the war on drugs, radical groups, control of resources and religious extremism. The use of space and cyber space has added a new dimension to conventional wars. As the battlefields merge, the wars of the future would also be conducted with energy, trade, and aid employed as weapons. Therefore, the very concept of national security needs to be re-examined.

War is distinct from conflict. The latter is a vast canvas and includes all shades of discord, involving both states and non-states. There are various instruments to address conflict. Here we will largely restrict ourselves to an exploration of one of those key instruments—military power, which, exercised by any entity, is the essential component of warfare, as war is specifically about employment of force to achieve a desired political end.

Conflicts remain a central element of the human condition. In some regions, traditional forms of conflicts have virtually disappeared while in others it remains a fact of everyday life. Yet there is a growing feeling in many parts of the world that the future nature of conflicts may be changing.

Technology is the driver of changes and this is no less so in warfare. What is less certain and easy to predict is how technology will develop and how it will be adapted to improve military capability. However, it would be safe to say that the future is unlikely to be a linear extension of present trends. Who could have predicted the impacts of social networking, the way it has shifted the balance between oppressive state regimes and their disaffected populace. In the terrorist attacks in the US on 11 September 2001, it was not a deceleration which enabled the terrorist operatives to attack the USA, but a combination of speed and slowness. The infrastructure of the side attacked was exploited by a clandestine group, which was able to go about preparing the attacks quietly and calmly, and then turned aircraft into missiles and jet fuel into explosive.

Wars of the future are likely to see an asymmetrical competition between high-technology and low-technology weapons. Since

11 September, we know that mere box cutter's knives, if used to hijack airlines so as to crash them into buildings and cities, can serve to shake a superpower to its foundations.

The arms race of the twenty-first century will no longer be symmetrical like those of the nineteenth and twentieth centuries, when Germany and England vied with each other in the construction of warships, or the USA and USSR in nuclear delivery systems. Yet, developed societies will have no choice but to pursue better and better technology just to remain capable of providing a military response to the growing diversity and sophistication in simplicity of the asymmetrical challenges we face.

Vulnerability of the Developed World. In principle, war has become not only politically but also economically unattractive for the developed countries. The costs outweigh the returns. In "post-heroic" societies, for whom the concept of self-sacrifice are no longer an ideal, the highest value is the preservation of human life and with it the multiplication and intensification of individual sensations of well-being. Developed societies have, therefore, justified every type of armament on the grounds of defence. The purpose of such a build-up is not to prepare for war but to prevent it.

Development theories that look forward optimistically to peace overlook the fact that through the socio-economic development of recent decades, new opportunities have arisen for profitable economies of developing countries based on war and violence. A world in which society has developed through interchange and cooperation is based on assumptions which can be taken for granted only if there is an extensive leveling out of the particularities stemming from religion, culture and civilization. Developed Nations cannot adopt asymmetric warfare as they are based on rule of law and political participation and will do their utmost to *avoid losses* in combat, which is possible only through superior military technology. The strategists of terror have recognized that "post-heroic" societies, with their lifestyle and self-assurance, are particularly vulnerable to attack by individuals who value martyrdom.

The De-Militarization of War. A return to the forms of war which the nationalization of warfare brought to an end during the 16th and 17th centuries and replaced by a disciplined military organization can already be observed. Civilian targets are now taking the place of military objectives, starting with towns and villages overrun and despoiled by militias and, warlords and extending to the symbols of political and economic might that were targeted in the US by terrorists in 2001. Suicide-bombers compensate for their military inferiority by giving up any chance of survival. A new perverse form of "heroism" has developed, which "post-heroic" societies are ill prepared to deal with from a military or psychological point of view.

Trends Visible in Recent Conflicts

The Second Lebanon War, 2006. In this war, Hezbollah was able to mix an organized political movement with decentralized military cells that employed adaptive tactics against a technologically superior enemy, the Israeli Defence Forces (IDF). Hezbollah used state like conventional military capabilities together with classic guerrilla tactics in a dense urban environment, whereas the Israelis followed plans intended for a conventional campaign. This led to a situation where, though much of the infrastructure inside Lebanon was destroyed, yet Hezbollah could claim victory.

The Russia-Georgia Campaign, 2008. The conflict began with escalation of a series of local clashes and sniper fire between Georgian Army troops and militia from the province of South Ossetia, which wanted to break away from Georgia and, together with another province Abkhazia, enjoyed Russian support. Russia responded with coordinated military operations and restored the situation in its favour, despite US backing and support to Georgia.

Sri Lankan–LTTE Conflict. The LTTE, which had grown in strength and reputation over three decades of fighting the Sri Lankan Army (SLA), made the mistake of engaging in positional warfare. As a result it was decimated and wiped out by the SLA, which adopted irregular tactics and means.

Operation Enduring Freedom. The experience in Afghanistan has clearly highlighted that while irregular forces/means cannot defeat conventional forces, they can patiently wear down and whittle political resolve. The importance of alliances and proxies has emerged loud and clear, as also the fact that modern armed forces need to continuously evolve and adapt to multi spectral challenges.

The Changing Nature of Conflict. Statistically, there are fewer conventional conflicts between states today, but intra-state conflicts have increased. Territorial disputes do exist and they can be cause for interstate conflicts. Internal and external securities are meshed today. More than ever before, Battles are, therefore, fought by irregulars and the police as well. Developments in weapons and equipment have given rise to new tactics and strategies. The military has a tougher job than ever before and has to be receptive to new ideas and adapt to changes faster.

In the last few decades, the enormous destructive power of strong conventional and nuclear capabilities has resulted in weaker states and non-state groups adopting sub-conventional and irregular means to achieve their political objectives. Conventional conflict is increasingly intertwined with sub-conventional conflict, with irregular forces using unconventional means and tactics. The irregular forces are becoming increasingly lethal, with access to technology and equipment that previously only conventional state forces could afford. The characteristics of future conflict can, thus, be summarised as under:

(a) The spectrum of conflict will range from conflicts between states to conflict with non-state actors and proxies.

(b) The boundaries between regular and irregular warfare are blurring. Even non-state actors are increasingly acquiring conventional capabilities that were earlier the exclusive preserve of nation states.

(c) Conventional conflict could either be preceded or succeeded by a period of irregular conflict, which would include low intensity conflict and stabilisation operations.

(d) Technology has empowered the individual and today, a single terrorist/guerrilla can cause severe damage to adversaries through cyber, financial and kinetic attacks, which earlier only large organisations or states could do. Future conflicts will demand concurrent investment in sharpening softer skills like cultural awareness training, language skills, psychological operations and human intelligence.

Sub-Conventional Conflict

States across the globe are increasingly involved in violent conflicts with non-state groups both within and across borders. Subversive forms of conflict are predominant. This is principally because of the limitations on other forms of warfare. Subversive threats to a nation's security can be domestic, externally supported, or externally fostered. The problem is exacerbated by the moral sanction that is accorded to external support to "freedom fighters" and "freedom struggles". Apart from terrorism, which is part of any insurgency, the world is witness today to the phenomenon of terrorist groups, driven by fanaticism and extremism, entrenched in sympathetic populations around the world, exploiting new technologies and globalisation to their advantage, and posing a threat to those they perceive as their enemies. Whereas such groups are unlikely ever to attain their abstract goals against resolute peoples and states, they are capable of causing extreme harm to civil society.

Sub-conventional wars are essentially wars between the weak and the strong. Such wars are fought for winning the political loyalty of the people and are people centric. The principal strategic challenge, thus, is to apply multiple means political, military, diplomatic, social, intelligence, informational and cultural to produce the desired strategic effect that will outcomes are determined by the staying power, reflected in political will and the ability to achieve the desired strategic effect by application of all means. Military force is a component of sub-conventional war, but not in terms of its destructive ability, which normally is the key in conventional wars.

Insurgency and terrorism are growing challenges on the global stage. In geographic terms, they are mostly rooted in the Asian continent but pose a threat globally, especially the developed powers. The ideological fuel and the motivating platform is often who religious extremism and is presently centered in the Afghanistan-Pakistan region. The Western choice of policy goals does not lie in the revision of assumptions regarding the nature of enemy, or attempts to improve their military effectiveness, but in an acceptance the conceptually, it is better to tackle insurgency and terrorism with indigenous efforts. In the context of counter-insurgency and terrorism, the Western strategic weaknesses in terms of war-fighting are characterised by:

(a) Over reliance on technology, firepower and conventional capability.
(b) Casualty aversion, exacerbated by the advent of the suicide

bomber and the remotely detonated Improvised Explosive Device (IED).

(c) Proclivity of the Western public to be impatient, resulting in constant weakening domestic support.

(d) Inability to field the large numbers of troops required.

When the Chinese president visited his counterpart in the White House during the heyday of the Bush administration, he brought with him some gift wrapped advice. While Bush was fighting an increasingly ferocious insurgency in Iraq, it was reported that Hu Jinta presented him with a copy of Sun Tzu's *The Art of War*. The point was subtle, but the allusion clear: while Bush had sent a conventional Army to Iraq to topple Saddam Hussein, other insurgents were waging another kind of war. With a rise in asymmetric conflict, armies must adapt and be prepared to meet and defeat the challenge posed by such adversaries. Inability or rather the impossibility, of bridging the cultural gap with the local population and, hence inability to win over the locals, makes the West unsuited for such wars in the Asian continent.

The Indian experience in counter insurgency and terrorism has been extensive, but the approaches to counter-insurgency and terrorism have been substantially different, especially in relation to the style of use of force and, more importantly, in leveraging the soft power of the armed forces. People centricity has been the bedrock of the Indian counter insurgency doctrine. Of course, each counter insurgency campaign will have its own mix of strategic vectors, with considerable contextual variations. But these differences do not detract from the principle of people centricity.

Technology has given lethality to small groups of people, especially with the advent of the suicide bomber and IEDS, but those groups, though seemingly tactically lethal, still require the support of the people, which they are deprived of, due to the indiscriminate application of their lethality with explosives. Ironically, their tactical success carries within it the seeds of strategic failure. From the strategic perspective, terrorism will remain a long-term nuisance, but it cannot succeed unless the counter terrorist reaction of the state converts it into an insurgency with significant popular support.

Hybrid Warfare

Hybrid warfare is a military strategy that blends conventional warfare, irregular warfare and cyber warfare. This approach to conflicts is a potent, complex variation of warfare. Hybrid warfare can be used to describe the flexible and complex dynamics of the battle space requiring a highly adaptable and resilient response.

Our current models for Counter terrorism and Counter insurgency are inadequate for the types of hybrid conflict that are likely in coming years. As Hezbollah's leader, Nasarallah put it after the 2006 war in Lebanon, "The resistance withstood the attack and fought back. It did not wage a guerrilla war either. It was not a regular army but was not a guerrilla in the traditional sense either. It was something in between. This is the new model."

Hybrid threat actors seek to master unrestricted operational art in order to reconcile overmatch and protect or advance their interests. The hybrid threat concept represents the evolution of operational art and a potential paradigm shift as a doctrinal and organizational Revolution in Military Affairs (RMA). Baptized in its modern form after the 1991 Gulf War, the hybrid threat construct is a sophisticated amalgam of unrestricted threat activities that have resisted codification. As an unrestricted collective methodology, the hybrid concept bypasses the cognitive boundaries of traditional threat characterization and the application of organized collective violence.

There is every likelihood that hybrid threat actors will increase the frequency and diversity of ways and means in the pursuit of their interests in coming decades. As such, the hybrid construct presents numerous implications for visualizing the future operational environment and for how militaries should formulate strategy, policy and resource investment priorities in the near future.

PART II: FORCE CAPABILITY DILEMMA

Characteristics of Future Conflict

Future conflict is likely to be characterized by the following:

(a) **Diverse Spectrum**: Conflicts will range from State versus State to State versus non-state or through Proxies.

(b) **Hybrid Wars.** The boundaries between regular and irregular warfare are blurring. Even non-state actors and groups are increasingly acquiring conventional capabilities that were earlier the exclusive preserve of Nation States.

(c) **Stabilisation Operations**. Such operations could involve operations in the reconstruction and social domains also.

(d) **Exploitation of Technology.** Technology will play a major role in determining the character of future conflicts, though the growing culture of technology has a weakening effect, in traditional military capabilities such as close combat and combat intelligence. Future Hybrid conflicts will demand concurrent investment in sharpening 'softer skills' like cultural awareness training, language skills and psychological operations.

Strategic Choices. What strategic choices do nation states have with respect to structuring their armed forces so as to adequately meet the challenge of likely future conflict? Strategic priorities for force development will be dictated by nature of threats faced by nation states and could be categorised as under:-

(a) **Nations with Land Threats and Unstable/Inimical Neighbours.** In cases where nation states have unsecured borders/inimical neighbours, the gravest threat to national security would be from a conventional conflict with the neighbouring state, even though the chances of a conventional conflict may be low. Higher on the probability scale of occurrence would be a threat from non-state actors working at the behest of inimical neighbours. The severity of threat in this case would be lower than in the conventional space. Therefore, planner's primary focus should be to prepare for the threat with the most serious consequences, at the same time catering for the force to adapt to handle threats from non-state actors. A typical example is India, which has to not only develop force structures for a conventional threat from Pakistan and China but also adapt to tackle proxy war and militancy in Kashmir and the North East.

(b) **Nations with no Direct Land Threat.** In this case, consequences of a state vs. state conflict (in the conventional sphere) are not so serious because there would be no direct threat to homeland security. Non-state actors would pose a more serious threat whether acting on their own or when backed by an inimical state. Force structure development, in this case, should focus on being prepared for non-state threat, however, still retaining the ability to adapt at short notice for a conventional state vs. state conflict. This is the model being adopted by the US and Western European militaries.

A force structure based on threat or capability alone may not be appropriate, and a balanced force based on both threat and capability would be a more prudent model. Each nation will have to adopt a choice based on a combination of the threats envisaged and capabilities desired.

Implications

(a) **Strong Conventional Capabilities.** The option of development strong conventional capabilities lends itself better for catering to threats across the entire spectrum of conflict. This is so because once conventional capabilities are in place the force needs only reorientation of mindset and specialised training to deal with sub-conventional conflicts, and this can be achieved in an acceptable time frame.

(b) **Strong Sub-Conventional Capabilities.** On the other hand, if emphasis is on developing strong sub-conventional capabilities to cater for immediate threat perception, then changing over for a conventional conflict may not be achieved in the defined time. This is so, because apart from reorientation capability development will take time.

It may be comparatively easier for a nation to achieve a defined conventional military capability given adequate resources and political will to do so. However, as future challenges and threats are likely to be hybrid in nature, there will be a need to develop strong sub-conventional and 4th generation warfare capabilities also, which in turn calls for a reorientation of mindset. This will itself be a significant challenge that will call for investment of considerable effort over time.

PART III: ADAPTING TO CHANGE

Role of Air Power

Recent military operations witnessed by the world give us a glimpse of how economical and precise they can be, if they are supported by air power. This is the emerging trend of air power, which is bound to be adopted by all nations, commensurate with their capabilities. Air forces can conduct deterrence, denial, coercion, decapitation and humanitarian missions. Perhaps the most important mission of these is the mission of deterrence. These forces make a potential enemy think twice before launching a pre-emptive strike, be it nuclear or conventional. The speed, range and flexibility of air forces give a nation the decisive advantage in achieving conventional deterrent value. Therefore, air power will continue to play a significant role in conventional conflict.

However, hybrid conflicts pose a challenge as to how air power can be best exploited and applied. In Lebanon in 2006, even though Israeli Defence Forces (IDF) fighters controlled the skies, Hezbollah was able to move men and equipment around the battlefield without significant hindrance. Use of air power in hybrid scenarios causes tremendous collateral damage, which undermines support for and legitimacy, of the effort. However, if orchestrated correctly, it can play substantial role in sub-conventional warfare and counterinsurgency operations. Airpower has the capability to erode an opponent's power, will and influence. It can enhance government legitimacy, projects national sovereignty into remote areas, accelerates a nation's overall development and provides an asymmetric advantage over adversaries. Some of its roles in sub-conventional sphere are:

(a) Provide political leaders immediate, unimpeded access to all territory to demonstrate governance and legitimacy by delivering goods, services, and humanitarian relief.
(b) Mitigate the traditional advantages of insurgents and terrorists: surprise, speed, stealth, manoeuvre, and initiative.
(c) Strengthen internal security mechanisms providing air mobility, aerial resupply, intelligence, surveillance and reconnaissance; command and control; and strike.
(d) Prevent insurgents from massing on the battlefield, and provides an option to strike them if they do.
(e) Patrol and assist in securing porous border areas and deny insurgents and terrorists sanctuary in ungoverned and remote areas.
(f) Complement and support the ground forces, which will remain the main pillar of the Nation's response to hybrid warfare.

The force structure mix for sub-conventional operations will be quite different from conventional operations. The dilemma, therefore, for air power will be whether to build capabilities for high end conventional operations or to develop capabilities and tactics to deal with the hybrid challenges of modern warfare. The jury is still out on this issue.

Role of Maritime Power

In an increasingly interdependent world, the value of effective maritime capability cannot be overstated. With the bulk of a nation's energy and trade routed across the seas and increasing interest in undersea natural resources, threats on the high seas have kept pace. Naval power will be essential for protecting our economic interests and extending humanitarian relief far beyond our shores. The Indian Navy is gearing up to give itself the capability to operate across the full spectrum of conflict from Low Intensity Maritime Operations to conventional war fighting to nuclear deterrence. In the conventional role the Navy would be expected to:

(a) Provide deterrence through threat of use of sea denial and sea control.

(b) Provide operational manoeuvre from the sea as also develop expeditionary capabilities.

(c) Carry out coercive diplomacy to safeguard national interests.

In keeping with India's emergence as responsible global player the navy will participate in maritime cooperation initiatives. These would include measures to insure protection of economic interests and Sea Lines of Communication, anti piracy operations, humanitarian assistance and disaster relief.

The Nuclear Dimension

With the development of nuclear capability, and the attendant danger of catastrophic use, there are differing perceptions on whether or not space remains for conventional conflict between nuclear powers. Since the 1998 nuclear tests, India and Pakistan have been through a limited war and a major military crisis, making clear that the nuclearisation of both the countries has not made conventional war between them an obsolete concept. Acquisition of nuclear weapon by Pakistan has not altered the strategic balance in the subcontinent and it has not been able to neutralise India's conventional war fighting superiority. Notwithstanding the nuclear deterrence in place, there is adequate strategic space for India to respond to a Pakistani misadventure, which might arise out of its miscalculated confidence. Nuclear capability may limit the objective, scope and intensity of war and despite views to the contrary, the nuclear threshold would not be as fragile and low as made out by many strategists and academicians.

Key take away which emerged after the Kargil War in 1999 were:

(a) Escalatory dynamics can in fact be controlled.
(b) Use of state sponsored proxies by Pakistan was exposed to the world.
(c) India's restrained response was globally appreciated.
(d) It was established that despite Pakistan's contrived nuclear irrationality, space remains for conventional conflict.

Conflict Dynamics with Reference to Non-State Players

The biggest concern for nation states is the acquisition of Weapons of Mass Destruction (WMD) by non-state actors. How will the dynamics of deterrence, coercion and escalatory control work against non-state actors? It is a nightmare scenario and remains a very real threat.

In order to be effective against non-state players, deterrence, coercion and escalatory control must rely on the following:

(a) International protocols to prevent proliferation through sanctions and other tough measures.
(b) Most important of all, international cooperation among intelligence agencies to detect moves by identified non-state actors to acquire WMD, so that timely counter action can be initiated.

Conclusion

Given the rate at which information technology is redefining human affairs, it is credible to believe that wars in the coming decades will leverage the very same technology, and its effect on the human condition, and will be quite different from anything we have seen in the past. Future wars will be hybrid and conventional forces. The world over will have to constantly adapt and evolve to face new challenges. Conventional conflicts are less likely, though there will always be space for limited warfare between nations, even against a nuclear backdrop, if vital interests are perceived to be at stake.

To effectively meet these hybrid and novel challenges, states must adopt an integrated approach towards developing all facets of comprehensive national power, which includes the socio-economic, political, cultural, environmental and military spheres. Military forces must be developed to be capable of safeguarding the national interests in line with emerging threats. The strategic choice is whether to prepare for the most dangerous, while adapting for the most likely, or prevail in today's wars and prepare to deter future conflicts. There is no easy answer.

Choices a nation makes or neglects to make, will be judged by posterity, however, the paradigm shift in the very concept of national security and hybrid nature of threats we will face in the coming years, demands that we understand the trends, even if the goal of war, in whatever form will always remain one of influencing people and organizations.

6

India's National Security Challenges in the Next Decade

Gen. Deepak Kapoor,
PVSM, AVSM, SM, VSM, ADC,
Chief of the Army Staff

Introduction

It gives me great pleasure to be amidst the faculty and students of Pune University to share my thoughts on **'India's National Security Challenges in the Next Decade'.**

Let me begin by flagging a few important issues with regard to our nation. India is a large country with a landmass of 3.3 million sq. km., a coastline of over 7,500 km. and an Exclusive Economic Zone of over 2 million sq. km. It has the second largest population and is the largest democracy in the world, comprising diverse ethnic, cultural and religious entities. The last two decades of economic reforms have resulted in the Indian economy growing rapidly, and today we are the fourth largest economy. India commands a unique geo-strategic location; a peninsula protruding into and dominating the Indian Ocean. We share land and sea borders with a large number of countries. Our strategic interests extend from South East Asia to Africa, the Middle East and the Central Asian Republics and we have legitimate concerns to developments in our extended neighbourhood, which influence our security calculus. As

India's regional aspirations grow, India will be expected to play a greater role in ensuring security and stability in the region.

Internally, we are in the midst of consolidating our societal structures and nation building. We wish to secure for ourselves a peaceful environment for achieving economic progress, technological development and prosperity. However, a country's desire for peace by itself is no guarantee for its security. We must have a clear understanding of the nature of threats to our security and should proactively counter both external and internal security challenges.

During my talk today, I would be covering issues related to **National Security Perspective, Threats to National Security and Management of National Security.**

NATIONAL SECURITY PERSPECTIVE

Concept of National Security and National Power

First, I think it imperative to put forward an understanding of the concept of national security. It encompasses the protection and promotion of national interests while avoiding or surmounting crises, conflicts and risks that have the potential to threaten national well-being. It implies prevailing in crises and conflicts, without suffering irreparable losses or sacrificing long-term national interests.

The traditional concept of security. The traditional concept of national security relates to the security of the State. It implies that the States alone have the right to protect their sovereignty and territorial integrity and those individuals must subordinate themselves to national interests. Until the end of the Cold War, the concept of national security was to ensure the protection of a nation from physical attacks and safeguarding its economic interests from devastating outside influences. State security was thus predominantly linked to the military dimension.

Emerging Concept of Security. And that brings us to the emerging concept of security. The modern state system endeavours to provide a secure space for progress of the individual and development of society. The security spectrum has, therefore, become more complex: It is no longer visualized in narrow military terms. How effectively a State is able to create an atmosphere for social and individual development, is what determines its potential to ensure security.

Determinants of National Security in the 21st Century. During the last two decades, there has been considerable emphasis on economic performance, human development and resilience of the state. With the emergence of trans-national forces and multi-national entities, state primacy has been diluted. Therefore, the foundations of national security rest on the social and economic well-being of the people. A socially fractious, economically backward and politically divided nation is unlikely to be militarily secure. Military security is a necessity, but not the only condition for national security. Therefore, a broader concept of national security in the 21st century encompasses five prongs—political stability, economic growth, diplomatic and military strength, societal development and environmental protection—as the determinants of security. Collectively this is referred to as Comprehensive National Power.

Comprehensive National Power (CNP). Security requires not only a desire, but also the capability to protect, nourish and strengthen national identity and assets. National assets, both tangible and intangible, could be grouped under two heads: primary assets which are vital for the existence, well-being and growth of a nation; and others, which contribute significantly to guarding, protecting and nurturing the primary assets. National security thus entails assessment and development of Comprehensive National Power, employing an integrated approach combining political, economic, military and other levers of both soft and hard power.

INDIA'S NATIONAL SECURITY PERSPECTIVE

With that, let us now dwell on India's National Security perspective.

Pillars of National Security. India's security policy flows from two cardinal principles: *one,* that we have no extra-territorial ambitions and two; we have no desire to transplant our ideology on others. India's strategic vision is in harmony with our traditional character as a peaceful, responsible nation that has abjured aggression and played a constructive, mainstream role in international relations.

Core Values. The core values that form the foundation of our Core National Interests are:

(a) Liberty, justice, equality, humanity, happiness, peace, prosperity and a healthy environment. Tolerance, assimilation and balance are manifest in the form of democratic, sovereign and secular governance.

(b) The others are the use of knowledge and technologies for establishing 'peaceful and economic growth'.

(c) Ensuring the fundamental rights of citizens as enshrined in the Constitution of India.

Core National Interests. India's core national interests, derived from our core values encompass **Political Independence**, which implies the continued existence as a sovereign, secular and democratic republic and the ability to chart an independent course in international relations; security, encompassing territorial integrity and unity, social harmony, internal peace and stability; **Development of Knowledge** for global integration; **Economic Prosperity; Development of Human Resources** by providing assured right to education, health, employment and human rights; environment protection by contributing towards growth and protection of natural resources and the fostering of an environment of peace and security conforming to India's national interests.

National Security Aim. Our National Security Aim is to 'ensure a conducive internal and external environment for unhindered economic progress and socio-political development, to enable India to assume its rightful place in the emerging world order'.

Having spelt out India's National Security Perspective, let us now consider what the threats/challenges to it are.

THREATS TO NATIONAL SECURITY

Paradigm shift in spectrum of conflict/employment of military power. Over the last couple of decades, we have seen distinctive changes in the nature of conflict. New threats are emerging and there is a paradigm shift in the manner they need to be countered. The emerging trends are:

(a) **Probability of conflict** using conventional military force between equal or near equal powers is receding, particularly among nuclear-capable nations.

(b) **Strategic/political** objectives are being sought to be attained more by coercive, deterrent and effect-based use of military power.

(c) Countries with strategic weapons and dual-use technologies seek to develop more robust capabilities, while denying the same to others.

(d) **Asymmetric warfare** has emerged as a formalised doctrine. Countries like Pakistan, North Korea and Syria have irregular forces as part of their war fighting machinery. There is a growing perception that the objectives of conventional war can also be attained through asymmetric/unconventional wars.

(e) **Irregular wars** are maximising the use of technology for achieving the strategic effects by tactical actions.

External Threats

The external threats facing India range from **traditional land-centric threats due to disputed borders** to **sub-conventional threats**, including their proxy war manifestations. Other security challenges arise from the spillover effects of a turbulent and unstable neighbourhood and a wide range of non-traditional threats.

Traditional land-centric threats: India shares approximately 3,323 km. of land borders with Pakistan and 3,488 km. with China, portions of which are unsettled. The situation along the Line of Actual Control with China has generally been peaceful, while the Line of Control and Actual Ground Position Line with Pakistan has witnessed periodic hostilities and an ongoing proxy war. Even though there are other areas of security concern, the unresolved border issues will continue to remain an important factor in our defence planning. I will now dwell on our relationship with Pakistan and China in some detail to enable you to get a better perspective of the nature of threats that we face.

Pakistan. The threat from Pakistan manifests in the form of **proxy war/ low-intensity conflict** as well as a **conventional threat**. While J&K is the main cause of conflict, hatred for India is so deeply engrained in the Pakistan psyche that it fails to see the benefits of cooperative engagement with India. Pakistan today presents a grim picture of a State in rapid decline. The current environment of political uncertainties, escalating militancy, violence, radicalisation of society and tribal complexities, severely undermines the state of Pakistan. The Mumbai terror attack and the responses thereafter have amply exposed Pakistan's complicity in its continued perpetration of state-sponsored terrorism in India. We, on our part, have to remain vigilant for such threats and be prepared to pre-empt as well as respond to such challenges. I can assure you that the Armed Forces will rise to this challenge and prevail over any threat to the nation's security.

China. Presently China is pursuing its long-term political goal of **developing its comprehensive national power**. Our multi-dimensional engagement with China is predicated on the recognition that these two rapidly developing and transforming nations need to come to terms with the rise of one another. It is in this context that bilateral relations, despite the unresolved border issue have strategically grown. Today, China is India's largest trading partner and we support each other on various issues such as preventing proliferation of nuclear weapons, energy security, WTO, global warming and the fight against terror. Improved bilateral ties will usher in peace and stability in the region. However, we need to take note of the likely implications of the improvement of infrastructure in Tibet, rapid modernisation of its armed forces, strategic initiatives in the Bay of Bengal and the Indian Ocean Region, proliferation of nuclear/missile technology to Pakistan and expanding military/ economic relationship with countries on our periphery, which could impact our security calculus in the long-term.

Other neighbours. Most of our other neighbours are undergoing some form of political transformation and experiencing varying levels of instability. This state of affairs is likely to continue for some time, be it the prevailing political brittleness and China' increasing footprints in Nepal, illegal migration from Bangladesh or the issue of resettlement and rehabilitation of over 2.7 lakh internally-displaced Tamils in Sri Lanka. **Events in neighbouring countries affect our security and require close monitoring**. All this calls for a continuous watch on the events around our periphery and ensure that there are no adverse spillover effects.

Maritime/regional challenges. Protecting India's trade and energy routes by securing sea lanes of communication, preventing maritime terrorism, piracy and ensuring the security of India's Diaspora in the Indian Ocean littoral countries are challenges that we are likely to face in the near future.

Asymmetrical and non-conventional threats. There are several asymmetric and non-conventional challenges, which transcend inter-state and inter-regional boundaries and require mutually acceptable solutions and coordinated efforts. Some of these include fundamentalism and violent extremism based on religion, caste, ethnicity or language; threat of use of 'weapons of mass destruction' by non-state actors; energy and water security; drug and human trafficking, proliferation of arms and counterfeit currency; vulnerability of computer networks and core institutions dependent on them—such as financial and banking systems; and, the internal social and political dimensions due to demographic shifts.

Non-state actors. The increasing role that non-state actors like Al-Qaeda or Lashkar-e-Taiba are playing in shaping global dynamics, have rendered traditional state boundaries less relevant. This is posing a serious challenge to state authority and leading to realignments in our neighbourhood.

Internal Threats

Internal Challenges. As you are aware, India's society is made up of diverse ethnic groups, cultures, languages and religious entities. This is both a strength and challenge. Although India's national integrity remains fundamentally secure, poverty, communalism, ethnic and religious diversity throw up various challenges from time to time. Internal security dynamics is worsened by a complex interplay of domestic, regional and international factors. There is also the challenge of inequitable distribution of wealth and resources.

Terrorism and Left-wing Extremism

(a) In **J&K**, there has been a **marked improvement** in the **security situation**. This is primarily because of the **'moral ascendancy'** gained over the terrorists by the security forces. Our focus on surgical operations based on hard Intelligence, causing minimum collateral damage and inconvenience to the local populace, is paying dividends. Despite the difficult circumstances, upholding human rights remains one of the cornerstones of our anti-terrorist operations. The growing stability in the State now necessitates focused socio-economic development.

(b) In the **North-eastern States**, relentless operations by the security forces have kept the situation well under control. Most parts of the region today are free of violence and normalcy has been restored. Sustained operational pressure and persuasion by the Security Forces has resulted in a large number of surrenders. Overall, we see that more and more groups are entering into **'Suspension of Operations'** agreements with the Government, which is a positive development.

(c) **Naxalism**. The increasingly disruptive activities of the Naxalites in the states of Chhattisgarh, Jharkhand, Odisha, Bihar, Madhya Pradesh, Andhra Pradesh and parts of Maharashtra, pose a major security challenge. The Government has adopted a multi-dimensional and integrated approach to counter this menace. Since it is primarily a socio-economic class struggle, the direct involvement of the Army is not mandated. The Army however, remains instrumental in strengthening State and Central Police forces by providing advice, training and rendering assistance in the establishment of counter-terrorism schools.

Lack of Opportunities—Youth Bulge. The world population is likely to grow from 6.1 billion in 2000 to around 8 billion in 2025. Ninety-five per cent of this increase is likely to take place in the less-developed parts of the world. This may lead to adverse consequences in less-developed countries. Moreover, while the population of countries around us like China is ageing we, on the other hand, have approximately 65 per cent people in the 15 to 55 year-age group. The creation of employment opportunities to channelise this large work force will be a formidable challenge in the future.

Religious Fundamentalism, Regionalism/Inter-state Disputes and Divisiveness in Society. Although India's national integrity remains fundamentally secure, pressures in terms of poverty, communalism, ethnic and religious diversity leading to divisions within society, will pose a major challenge. Governance in a number of states will require considerable improvement to counter these challenges.

Other Challenges

Economic Disparity. Our economy is growing at a respectable rate. We have large untapped natural resources and are recognised as a potential technological powerhouse. It is believed that we may overtake Japan in terms of GDP within the next decade. Concurrently, the number of people living below the poverty line is high and may be to the tune of 250-350 million! Abject poverty and not being able to assure inclusive growth would be a challenge that affects our national security.

Resource Scarcity. National, economic and energy security are inextricably linked. To meet growing demands, there is increased competition for control of energy resources amongst global players. It is anticipated that by 2025, energy scarcity will be the driving factor in regional and global geo-politics. This has the potential of leading to **'confrontation and conflicts'**.

Global Frameworks/Institutions. The trend towards greater diffusion of authority and power that has been on the rise in recent past is likely to continue, due to the emergence of new global power equations, potential expansion of regional blocs and enhanced strength of non-state actors and networks. The multiplicity of actors on the international scene with their own vested interests has the potential to fragment the international system and incapacitate international cooperation.

Miscellaneous, Differing ideologies, denial of advance and dual-use technologies to lesser developed nations, economic and trade embargoes, extension of territorial disputes to maritime and space, and cyber transparency versus need for privacy, are various areas of conflicting interests that are shaping the attitudes and response of nations in framing their security strategies.

Having covered the threats to our country's security, let us now move on to approaches for management of the same.

MANAGEMENT OF NATIONAL SECURITY

Threats and vulnerabilities are complex and diverse. All elements of state power will need to develop strategies, capacities and capabilities to counter them. A synergised strategy encompassing political, diplomatic, economic, military and internal security dimensions is the foremost deduction. Strategy so evolved should be bench-marked against our more enduring core values and core national interests.

Recommended Approach

(a) **Need for articulating a long-term perspective for national security**. India's role, as a stabilising power in the region, is getting increasingly recognised. A well-orchestrated and calibrated employment of the Armed Forces to further the nation's foreign policy must be seen as a potent tool of comprehensive national power. Towards this end, a holistic approach to national security requires seamless coordination between various stakeholders, i.e., the ministries of the Government. Requisite interface needs to be institutionalised, on priority. The National Security Council Secretariat is working towards developing a National Security Doctrine to articulate a long-term perspective for national security.

(b) **National consensus on core issues**. In the strategic realms, we need to **foster national consensus on matters related to national security, which demonstrates a collective national will** in responding to events that threaten our interests and sovereignty. This was amply demonstrated during the Kargil conflict and the recent Mumbai terrorist attack. Further, consensus promotes nationalism and gives the requisite legitimacy to the nation in charting its future course of action.

(c) **Develop better intelligence capabilities and synergy among intelligence agencies**. There is an overarching need to integrate the Intelligence agencies of the ministries of Defence, Home, Finance, Space, Atomic Energy, Information Technology, Agriculture, Health and Transportation for synergizing their effort in tracking, gathering, collating and disseminating actionable intelligence both at the strategic and tactical levels. The establishment of a 'Multi-Agency Centre' under the Intelligence Bureau is a step forward in this direction.

(d) **Modernisation of the police and para-military forces**. In order to meet the internal security challenges posed by militancy, insurgency, terrorist organisations and Naxals in various parts of our country, there is an inescapable need to train and suitably equip the Police and CPO forces to effectively meet these challenges. The tendency to resort to manpower accretions without matching modernisation will be counterproductive. The raising of specialist units like the Greyhound and COBRA units, to conduct operations against Left-wing extremists (Naxals) is a step in the right direction.

(e) **Greater leverage of our military strength**. Diplomacy is an effective instrument in soft power leverages. Participation in UN-sponsored peace missions, anti-sea piracy operations and disaster relief are some activities that project a nation's image in international fora. India needs to continue to play a constructive role in them. With our immediate neighbours, we need to develop a strong military-to-military cooperation primarily to assuage their apprehensions of our intent and minimise the growing influence of our potential adversaries. I need to assure this knowledgeable audience that necessary steps have been instituted in this regard.

(f) Management of Immediate and Strategic Neighbourhood

(i) There is a need to evolve a comprehensive approach for positive engagement with our immediate and strategic neighbourhood. Towards this end, a collective approach will need to be evolved, to include all the stakeholders including the Ministry of Defence, for policy formulation.

(ii) We also need to ensure benign and cooperative neighbours by making them partners and stakeholders in achieving mutual economic growth and development through integrated and inter-dependent economies.

(g) Technology. Technology is likely to play an important role in any form of conflict in the coming decades. There is a requirement to set-up a Defence Technologies Commission to oversee technology development for the Armed Forces and ensure that the vulnerability of the nation to technology denial regimes of various kinds is reduced. The need of the hour is to reduce our dependence on foreign technology.

(h) Perception management. Wars are deterred, won or lost in the minds of a country's national leadership which gets influenced by domestic and international public perceptions. Steps must be taken to shed India's image as a soft power state. Sound psychological and information operations themes propagated through diplomacy, Diaspora, media and cyber space coupled with credible demonstration of soft and hard power should project India's political will to respond resolutely and effectively for safeguarding of our national interests.

CONCLUSION

Our nation faces many challenges that are well known. National security is to do with a nation's well-being. I believe that the time is right for us to move forward towards building a strong nation. With greater participation of the people in our democracy, it would promote a greater sense of belonging, a sense of ownership and commitment, which as a combined whole shall reflect the spirit of a new emerging India.

I wish to conclude on an optimistic note. **Our strategic location in the subcontinent, our size and status has given us a unique opportunity to play an important role in the emerging global order**. Our rising capability has drawn us closer to other nations of the world and is encouraging us to take on greater responsibilities. We need to **ensure prosperity and growth in the region as also project the country as a responsible state that is ready and willing to shoulder this responsibility with élan and pride**.

Thank you.

7

The Emergence of the Indian Air Force as a Strategic Aerospace Power

Air Chief Marshal F.H. Major,
PVSM, AVSM, SC, VSM, ADC,
Chief of the Air Staff

Introduction

As a long-time instructor at the Armoured Corps School and Centre and at the College of Combat, Gen. Joshi had understood the importance of developing a strategic vision, through rigorous study and critical analysis; A thinking General, he encouraged and gave impetus to the systematic study of national security. A widespread and informed discussion on issues of national security amongst all Indians was his dream. His emphasis on the cultivation of a strategic culture is apparent from his endowments and creation of chairs for academic excellence in policy and strategic studies. It is, therefore, indeed appropriate that we carry his dream forward in such a manner.

Strategic Thought

Our country has remained under some form of foreign yoke for most of its recent existence. I speak of the past three centuries. Such a state has obviously precluded any kind of original strategic thought, for the very simple reason, that "there simply was no need". It is only since independence, that we have become conscious of our identity as a nation, and the responsibility of our own destiny. It is the dawn of this awareness that marks the beginning of Indian strategic thought.

There is a considerable amount of recorded strategic thought in the West. Land and sea warfare, being the traditional modes through which nations exerted their will, were systematically researched. Clausewitz, Jiminy, Alfred Mahan, du Pica and many others analysed the nature of war and its use as a means of coercion.

The use of airpower, being relatively recent, suffered from a notable lack of recorded thought. I must also admit that airmen are mostly "doers" and neglected serious and analytical thought. Very little was known or studied about the application of airpower. There were some attempts from the likes of Douhet, Trenchard, Slessor and Boyd, but they and their views remained obscure for a long time. One should note that until recently most theorists around the world tended to equate strategic bombing with strategic airpower. That they are different, I will come to later.

It is in this context that today I will acquaint you all with, **"The Emergence of the Indian Air Force as a Strategic Aerospace Power".** As students of defence and strategic studies, I am sure that the shape and objectives of the future IAF would interest you.

THE ENVIRONMENT

Let me begin by summarising the major influences that govern our geopolitical environment currently. Change seems to be the order of the day, with the past three decades having seen an upheaval of the established world order. From a bipolar world with clearly polarised alliances, we were briefly reduced to a uni-polar one and now we seem to be towards multi-centricity. The day of the global village is truly here. The recent crisis in the global financial markets reinforces this view. In such a scenario, no nation can remain insular or immune to any development anywhere on the globe. Nation-states actively interact with each other on the world stage in a number of ways and each seeks to control the sequence of events to their advantage.

National Power

Manipulation of events, in order to achieve one's objectives, is the intention of national strategy. Economic influence, diplomatic advantage, information superiority, military prowess and the quality of its citizens are some of the major elements of national power. The effect would be obviously magnified if all these elements could be used in concert, in an appropriate mix, directed intelligently by a central authority. That is the essence of national strategy. Don't you think that it is time that India had some form of an all-encompassing strategy that could be used to attain its objectives?

Military force is one of the more visible ingredients of national power that has traditionally been used by nations in a number of ways in order to secure their national interests. Let me tell you that Aerospace power today possesses immense capacity to exert influence across the entire spectrum from outright coercion to building friendships.

Why do we need the Indian Air Force? What capacity and potential must the IAF have? I am sure questions like these may have troubled you at some time or the other. By the time I finish, I hope to acquaint you with the immense capability that aerospace power provides to our national leadership and how it can be used to achieve national objectives in conjunction with other elements.

Before 1 proceed further, it would be worthwhile to re-examine our national aspirations. What has really changed between 1971 and 1998? In the years after independence, whilst we were coming to terms with our identity, whilst still pursuing an illusory ideal world, we remained a predominantly pacifist State. We still are! But in recent times our economic resurgence, increase in our collective confidence and inherent capability has made us look towards enlarging our area of influence. This fact is a natural progression of our growing stature, and it is in this context that the Indian Air Force aspires to develop a capability that can safeguard national interests at the extremities and facilitate growing national aspirations.

NATURE OF CONFLICT

Coming back to a more fundamental level, as students of strategy and military studies, I am sure that you understand the full impact of the

Clausewitsian premise that "War is but a continuation of politics by other means". The world that we live in is a turbulent one and conflict has been a constant throughout our recorded history. As students of the pragmatic nature of international relations, you will agree with me when I say that, "Conflict in some form or the other is inevitable amongst humans and a peaceful, harmonious world seems to be more of a utopian ideal".

Though a constant, I would like to submit that the very nature of conflict itself changes and evolves with time and technology. The latter half of the twentieth century has seen major changes come about in the nature and conduct of warfare. The days of total wars, with standing armies slugging it out face to face, over protracted periods are unlikely. The nuclear factor, emergence of non-state actors, asymmetric confrontation, increased economic interdependence, world opinion, media activism, etc., have resulted in an almost total transmutation of armed conflicts. The International Human Rights Law and the Laws of Armed Conflict have in their own way made the protagonists in armed conflicts more answerable. Therefore, in my view, future conflicts are most likely to be limited in scope, time and space, but they would be prosecuted at high technological and even higher intensity levels.

Your research and study would have made it amply clear that in order to maintain stability and equilibrium in our neighbourhood, it is essential for our country to possess a strong military force. By saying that, I am not for a moment advocating any kind of aggressive tendencies. But, a serious study of the balance of power equations amongst States makes it amply clear that "Only credible deterrence can be an effective stabiliser".

OUR NEIGHBOURHOOD

With that preamble, let me now talk about the situation in our neighbourhood. Analysis of our environment is essential if we are to make any assumptions that will dictate our security needs. To the west and north-west of us, Iraq and Afghanistan continue to simmer with ongoing conflicts. The Central Asian States remain turbulent with increasing instability as they come to terms with the decline of the erstwhile USSR and the emergence of the new Russia. Closer home, Pakistan, which now has a new democratic government installed, remains a source of concern to all of us. Nepal is just coming to terms with a new form of governance and remains susceptible to violence. China plays a strategic game and seeks to be the regional power, competing with India in every sphere.

Nuclear Dimension

There are many other issues that dictate our actions and define the boundaries within which we have to operate. The most visible and important factor that undermines all our relationships is, that of the "nuclear dimension". The fact that our neighbourhood has nuclear capability and long-range delivery platforms introduces a very dynamic variable in our relations.

Borders

The next issue that contributes to friction in South Asia is a legacy from our colonial past and that is the emotive issue of unresolved borders. India shares long borders with a number of countries and there are small pockets and areas that still remain contested. They remain zones of stress and will continue to be a potential source of conflict until such time a settlement is reached.

Terrorism

India has also faced the threat of terrorism for a very long time and has grappled with it long before it was even thought of or recognised in the West. The threat is now mutating into newer forms and methods and to deal with this unconventional threat on a daily basis, our Armed Forces and Para-military Forces are more active than ever before.

Scale of Conflict

Whilst we do advocate peaceful co-existence, it would be quite apparent to you that we face threats from across the entire spectrum of conflict—from low intensity border conflicts to full scale nuclear war. Our neighbours continue to arm and equip themselves with the sole aim of targeting India. Pakistan makes no secret of its plans to acquire Kashmir and split our country. Chins lays claim to large portions of our territory and uses them to raise the ante in accordance with its larger design.

Based on these realities, it must be apparent to all you scholars that in the last two decades, our national security needs have undergone radical changes. Whilst the need to defend our territory and project a suitable deterrent posture remains, India simultaneously also seeks a greater role for itself on the world stage. Consequently, the Indian Air Force's outlook too has undergone a change from being 'Neighbour-centric' to a possible Regional Force'.

AIRPOWER

This learned audience is fully aware of the profound influence that aerospace power has had in shaping the modern world. The increasing capability of airpower and its unique attributes make it a very attractive method of addressing conflict situations. Precision, Stealth, Ubiquity and Reach, now create a wide range of possibilities that open up an exciting array of employment options. This immense flexibility and variety makes aerospace power the natural instrument of choice in conventional as well as unconventional conflict scenarios, as well as force projection.

My Vision of Future Operations

Keeping in mind the prevalent strategic compulsions and likely engagements in the future, I would like to present to you my views on the conduct of future operations. I think that, conflicts in the future are likely to be short and sharp, conducted simultaneously at all levels and against a variety of objectives. The intensity of operations will be extremely high with precision, smartly delivered ordnance and with control over escalation and disengagement.

Present Plan of Acquisition

In order to acquire our envisaged potential, the Indian Air Force is in the process of a very comprehensive and focused modernisation programme. We are at varying stages in the induction of a wide range of equipment, which includes all types of aircraft, weapons, missiles, sensors, communication equipment, etc. We are even upgrading our field infrastructure, laboratories and maintenance facilities. The scale is simply immense. You must have read and heard a great deal about it because it has drawn considerable media attention.

We are going about this process in a very systematic and methodical manner. We have defined the capability that we would like to have by the end of the 13th Plan period, i.e., by 2022. Based on this requirement we are acquiring our assets in a phased manner so as to acquire the desired capabilities. For example, to achieve the capability to project power at a distance, i.e., 'Strategic Reach', we would need combat platforms that can reach there. We would need Air-to-Air Refuellers and AWACS (Airborne Warning and Control Systems) to operate over a distant region. To be effective there, we would need robust Communication and Command & Control systems. We would need airlift, maintenance and logistics to sustain our effort. So, as you can see, our acquisitions are not simply in isolation but are holistic and are meant to address specific needs. Similar is the case with our Air Defence and many other facets of operations.

STRATEGIC NATURE OF AIRPOWER

Having shown you what the future IAF would look like, I want to highlight one aspect that is very unique to airpower, which I mentioned earlier, and that is its strategic nature. The lines between tactical or strategic platforms blur dramatically. It is the effect that is strategic or tactical. Aerospace power does not have to be always used for destruction alone.

Seemingly isolated actions of an airman can have far-reaching strategic implications. I would go so far as to say that every action or inaction of an element of airpower has ramifications on national policy. The Berlin Airlift was a strategic use of airpower without firing a single shot. Very often, simple re-positioning of combat assets or presence over an area can have an effect.

We all recognise that, the decision to use airpower in any situation makes a very powerful statement. In our own recent context, whilst the Kargil incursions were definitely news, they grabbed world attention only when airpower was used. Such an act invariably demonstrates the resolve of the political leadership. Interestingly, a very different effect was illustrated with the Indian Air Force action of not crossing the LoC. It may be argued that such an act, one that demonstrated restraint, in contradiction to tactical propriety, paid greater dividends in the form of gaining favour in world opinion and ultimate achievement of our national objective, that of evicting the intruders.

These are simple examples that I use to illustrate the point that I am trying to make. A thorough understanding of the application of aerospace power and its synergistic use with other elements of national power can create a very powerful national strategic influence.

CONTRIBUTION OF AEROSPACE POWER: IAF

Let me now dwell a bit on the contribution of aerospace power with specific reference to the IAF, in furthering our relations with other countries. After long decades of seclusion, it was only around 2004 that the IAF re-initiated interaction with foreign Air Forces and made its presence felt on the international stage. In the past four to five years, the IAF has participated in bilateral and multilateral exercises in the USA, South Africa, France, UK, Singapore, UAE, and with many others in India. The professionalism of the IAF is now recognised the world over.

We have just returned from Exercise 'Red Flag' held at Nellis in the USA. We participated with a contingent of Su-30MKIs, IL-78 Air-to-Air Refuellers, IL-76 transport aircraft and a small "Garud" Special Force. 'Red Flag' is a very complex operational level exercise, usually for NATO countries only. We acquitted ourselves very well earning professional admiration.

Friendly countries seek to increase interaction and are keen to share our experience and expertise. Even as I speak now, an IAF team of pilots and technicians train RMAF (Royal Malaysian Air Force) personnel and assist them in the induction of their Su-30MKM. This is our way of building bridges of friendship and opening avenues of goodwill. Our 'Sarang' Helicopter Display Team carried out more than 35 displays in Europe and the UK earning the title of the 'Best Looking Close Formation Team' at the Berlin Air Show. Our 'Surya Kiran Aerobatic Team' has just performed at the Zhuhai Air Show in China for which I was also invited. These bonds of friendship coupled with the fact that we are a credible force in being, makes the IAF a fine foreign policy brand ambassador!

United Nations

We also stand fast in our commitment to the United Nations. We are one of the largest contributors of peacekeeping forces—over 9,000 troops. Presently, the IAF has contingents of medium-lift and attack helicopters in Africa, and they continue to provide significant assistance in maintaining and enforcing peace in some of the unfortunate strife-torn regions in Congo and Sudan.

Humanitarian Aid

Our Air Force has more often than not been the public face of mercy and relief on countless occasions. It has invariably been the first on the scene, bringing relief during many disasters. Today the IAF has 'Reach'. Within 48 hours of Hurricane "Katrina" striking mainland USA and after the recent Chinese earthquake, IAF IL-76s' were landing at New Orleans and Chengdu with relief material.

Let me give you another example of how a combination of elements of national power enhanced India's international stature. Devastated by a cyclone and floods and stung by international ostracism, Myanmar refused all foreign aid except India's. Deft diplomatic manoeuvring, coupled with speedy transport of relief by IAF IL-76s and AN-32s, demonstrated India's capability and influence in the neighbourhood. That is a strategic achievement.

Strategic influence can be exerted only if there is credibility. Credibility, very simply means, "the capability to carry out what you promise". On the international stage, you would be taken seriously only if you have demonstrated capability. Just as how the Indian Navy foiled an attempt at piracy, off the Somalia coast; demonstrating Reach and Projection of credible aerospace power at any point, is a strategic statement. Those Air Force Exercises on different continents, that I mentioned earlier, give out a subtle message that is understood by the concerned observers. The message is: the IAF can project power, quickly and effectively, wherever and whenever!

CHALLENGES

Let me now return to something that you as students of national security should be aware of. Whilst we are in the process of acquiring new capabilities and are amidst a transformation, we also have a few challenges that occupy me and my Staff in Air Headquarters.

Managing the Change

The first of these is to manage our organisation during this phase. You must understand that no force in the world can consist of only modern equipment. There will always be a mix of old, current and modern equipment with which we have to continue to operate. Most of our equipment is being phased out, upgraded or replaced. Legacy platforms and their maintenance systems have to co-exist with state-of-the-art modern practices. The same goes for training and combat employment as well. We also have contrasting technologies of Western fleets alongside Russian designs. All these have created a great operational, maintenance, training and doctrinal upheaval, which I have to manage. I know that if we do it right now, then we would have laid the foundations of a very competent Air Force of the future.

The New Battle Space

As I mentioned earlier, new technologies have unarguably changed the way we operate. The capabilities that advancements in technology provide also generate some vulnerability. The very factor responsible for increasing one's capability naturally becomes a target for the adversary.

Let me elaborate. Aerial combat has changed drastically in the past few decades. From close-range aerial combat involving guns, the environment is now dominated by extremely long-range sensors and weapon systems, which are orchestrated by complex networks and fast moving intelligence. This has created new centres of gravity and targets of a different kind. Space, Cyberspace and Information Warfare are the new zones of conflict, and we are in the process of developing doctrines, structures, tactics and expertise to dominate this new arena. Adapting and preparing the IAF combat to this new battle space is my next challenge.

Integration of Space

Our plans for future expansion have made it inevitable that we would have to utilise the realm of **space**. In my view, Space is an integral part of air operations. Whilst I am not a die-hard proponent of the weaponisation of space, I am convinced that harnessing the capabilities that space provides creates a force multiplier effect and increases the effectiveness of our operations manifold. India has a well-developed space programme and great latent capability in this domain. Until now, however, the products have largely been for civilian users. It is my intention to harness the capability that space-based assets provide, and put in place structures and mechanisms, so as to exploit the enhanced capability.

Joint Warfare

Till now I have spoken only about the capability of the IAF and its role as an aerospace power, As students of security, strategy and military studies, you would be right in wondering whether the IAF is planning all this in isolation. Let me assure you on that count—No! Our plans are based on national objectives and must be used in consonance with all other elements of national power, be they land, sea, diplomatic, economic, or media. We have made our acquisitions to bolster our joint capability, so that we enhance our overall effectiveness. It is my view that, the most appropriate mix of power must be used to achieve the desired objective. The combination would vary with each situation and capability.

Whilst it has occupied Western minds in recent years, let me tell you that we in our own unique way have always been 'Joint'. Jointness is not a new concept for the Indian Armed Forces. If you recall, on 27 October 1947, a fledgling Air Force and a nascent Army stopped the Pakistani advance into J&K. That was a classic Joint Operation. We have had wonderful institutions like the NDA here and the Staff College in Wellington, which have always been joint. In fact the Western world is getting around to it now. You must appreciate that our method of operations **must** suit our unique circumstances. We must develop our individual core competencies, and design mechanisms to plan, train and execute operations that utilise these individual strengths.

CONCLUSION

As I approach the end of my talk, I want you to appreciate that the shape and application of aerospace power is governed by a large number of intangibles. The geo-political compulsions, economic and political realities, foreign policy, national 'ill', all will dictate the growth of aerospace power. What the future holds can only be a form of educated crystal gazing. Would the emphasis shift to unmanned vehicles, or would it all shifts to space? Will battles be fought in the virtual domain and will there be new centres of gravity?

Since the German attack on Poland in 1939, no country has won a war in the face of enemy air superiority. Conversely, no state has lost a war while it maintained air superiority. It remains an unalterable fact that whoever controls the air, generally controls the surface.

Aerospace capabilities of a nation undoubtedly form one of the major strands of its strategic posture. Control and superiority in this sphere, not necessarily in direct conflict, automatically places a nation in a position of pre-eminence, giving it strategic power.

It is our mandate to provide our leadership with an array of response options. The questions of when, where, why and how to use aerospace power will continue to torment military and political strategists in the future. A thorough understanding of the principles of airpower and its applications are essential. I thank the University of Pune and the Department of Defence Studies, for giving me this opportunity to share some of my thoughts with you.

Jai Hind

8

Role of the IAF in the Changing Regional Security Environment

Air Chief Marshal S.P. Tyagi,
PVSM, AVSM, VSM, ADC,
Chief of the Air Staff

GEOPOLITICAL AND SECURITY ENVIRONMENT

International World Order

The last decade and a half has been characterized by many changes. The end of the cold war and the 9/11 terrorist attack have brought about a greater international convergence on global security issues and challenges. While significant differences of perception remain, there has been a change in diplomatic and power equations around the world. Old confrontations have given way to new equations and alignments. Globalization aided by technology is linking economies and is seriously challenging the traditional 'nation-state' concept. Economic and national interests, rather than ideology, are shaping international interests. Increased disparity in economic and military power amongst the big and small states has resulted in a large number of dissatisfied states. It has brought about changes in the realistic understanding of inter-state relations.

While the world is presently uni-polar this, I think, is a transient stage. In a decade or two, the world order will stabilize into a multi-polar environment. Major players will be the USA, the EU, Brazil, China, Russia, Japan and India. The war in Iraq has altered many equations in the Middle East influencing our own foreign policy. Similarly, proliferation and standoff over Iran and North Korea have affected several diplomatic alignments. What is of direct concern to us is the Asian region. The last few decades have witnessed the rise of Asia as a major power centre in the new world order, an order that is characterized by 'geo-economics' overshadowing 'geo-politics'. This area is also characterized by being the sole region with a nuclear flash point, a region in which three nuclear capable nations have been active adversaries for decades.

South Asia and the Indian Ocean Region

India has a geographical advantage because of its prominent position in South Asia. We are a rapidly growing economic power that enjoys strategic relationships with several countries. Besides, we are a recognized hub of expertise in IT software and have a substantial English-speaking populace. This gives us a unique opportunity to play an important role in the emerging global order with special reference to the South-Asian region. We stand in this region as a beacon of democracy amongst a multitude of human diversities and economic disparities. In terms of size, population, levels of development, technology and military power, we are far ahead of our neighbours. This has in the past resulted in apprehensions of hegemonic tendencies in the minds of some of our neighbours. We need to dispel these fears through confidence building measures.

Over the last two decades, India has recorded an average annual growth rate of 6 per cent. It is now the fourth largest economy in the world in terms of purchasing power parity. The size (GDP) of the economy has doubled since 1991, and is expected to redouble by 2010. This has made our country more and more energy-hungry. Beyond our immediate region, we have vital interests in the Gulf and South-East Asia. Being an important source of energy, the Gulf forms part of our strategic neighbourhood. Besides, it is the home to over 3.5 million Indians and is a major trading partner.

The requirement of strategic space to influence this region has long been the policy of major powers. As a result, South-Asia and the Indian Ocean Region (IOR) have seen an increase in global activity in recent years. The IOR has been a recognized vortex of activity for decades. It holds the bulk of the world's oil, gas, mineral and fishery resources, and is thus an attractive venue for many players. It is against this backdrop that India's strategic location in South Asia and the Indian Ocean is of paramount importance. The need to guarantee security of energy sources and sea-lanes in the IOR would therefore be a prerequisite to ensure the unhampered growth of our economy. One can therefore surmise that our areas of security concern have expanded far beyond the geographical borders of our nation-state. The area of security encompasses Sumatra on the African Coast on the east-west axis, and from Central Asia including the CAR countries to the Antarctica on the north-south axis.

Threat Assessment

Whilst there have been several positive developments in our relations with Pakistan over the last year-and-a-half, we cannot assume that the peace process is firmly entrenched. Terrorist threats and attacks continue to be a regular phenomenon indicating that the infrastructure for terrorism in Pakistan and POK is still very active. Pakistan continues to make repeated and unacceptable demands besides raising the Kashmir issue whenever it can. Fortunately, our own standing in the international forum as a responsible nuclear power with an impeccable record in proliferation continues to grow. We are demonstrating a growing capability to shoulder regional and global responsibilities.

China, while not an immediate threat, has a booming economy and is rapidly modernizing her armed forces. It is more likely to view us as a regional economic threat, and perhaps will be forced to attempt to stem our growth and influence in this region. China's strategic encirclement of our country is already well under way and this would only lead to more problems for us in the future. Another aspect to consider is that China would not like to see its Asian peers, Japan and India, joining the UN Security Council's permanent membership. Thus in opposing Tokyo's bid, China would automatically ensure that India's candidacy is denied.

In an environment of uncertainties as regards our neighbours, India has to cater to the full spectrum of threat, from low-intensity conflicts

(LIC) and proxy wars to all-out wars and even nuclear wars. There has been no linear concept of escalation in this region. There is a need to strike a balance between the credibility of deterrence through threats, and risk management through implementation of safeguards. Prolonged hostility has generated a greater potential for misunderstanding. We need to maintain a high level of vigilance and defence preparedness. Our preparedness would need to take into account all sorts of contingencies, including out-of-area operations, for containment of foreign influence in the South Asia and IOR regions.

Another area of concern that is fast influencing military strategy is "non-traditional' threats to national security. Threats to human ecology are fast expanding. Issues like water scarcity; rising population and its migration and global dependency on energy resources, will all give rise to new areas of conflict. Our forces would also have to deal with degradation of strategic security infrastructure caused by unforeseen natural calamities. We are witness to the recent earthquake in the border areas of J&K. Similarly, the floods that ravaged many of our states, the snow blockade in J&K and the tsunami, have all seen the armed forces being drawn into to play a very active and dominant role in providing relief operations. Our involvement also extends to reaching out to other countries in times of crisis as was done during the tsunami and Hurricane Katrina. In catering for these contingencies, the armed forces need to reorganize, equip, and be trained for such eventualities. The Armed Forces need a comprehensive joint approach to be able to defend not only national interests, but also exercise their influence on traditional and non-traditional threats. In consonance with the perceived requirement, the need to equip our forces with tools of strategic reach is essential.

India's Response

Our country's response to external threats and challenges has always been restrained, measured and moderate, consistent with a peaceful outlook and a reputation as a peace-loving country. Pursuit of economic goals must be our top priority. We are living in an era of globalization, and would perforce need to forge strategic partnerships with major players. Whilst diplomacy must remain our foremost means of dealing with challenges related to security, there could be no worthwhile development without security. In other words, we need to retain a strong military power. Therefore, it is essential that we identify our national security strategy from which would flow our military strategy to safeguard our national interests. There is, thus, a pressing need for a clearly enunciated national strategic vision for the armed forces spanning the next 15-20 years.

THE IAF'S INVOLVEMENT IN WARS SINCE INDEPENDENCE

Having covered the geopolitical and security environment, I will now dwell on the IAF's role in this security matrix. I will begin by tracing the role played by the IAF in the wars and campaigns since independence.

War in 1947-48. In 1947, Pakistani invading guerrilla forces had reached the outskirts of the capital of Jammu and Kashmir, Srinagar by the time the ruler acceded to India on 26 October 1947. On the same day, Air Force and civilian Dakotas flew troops from Delhi to Srinagar. The timely use of non-combat air power played a crucial role in relocating ground forces, which were subsequently able to push back the invading guerrilla forces. Similarly, the attempt to capture Leh by the Pakistan Army was thwarted by timely, and what has become a legendary airlift, by Air Commodore "Baba" Meher Singh.

1962 War with China. The debacle in 1962 is well known. This is the only war that we lost after Independence. Significantly, this also happens to be the only war in which combat air power was never utilized. Perhaps, if combat air power had been used, the outcome of the war could have been different.

1965 War. In the 1965 War, the Air Force came into play only on the 1 September when Pakistan launched a major land offensive with air support in the Jammu sector. India was caught unprepared as the Pakistani armour thrust towards the key town of Akhnoor. The Indian Army asked for air support. Our Mystere aircraft were able to stop the armour well short of Akhnoor. From then on, the guerrilla war was completely overtaken by a regular war between the two militaries that finally ended in a ceasefire. Once again, air power played an important role in warding off the Pakistani offensive.

1971 Operations. In the 1971 operations, the IAF was able to achieve air superiority in the Eastern Sector within a matter of a few days. The Tangail battalion drop followed this. Air power was thus put to good use.

Kargil Operations. During the Kargil operations, supply camps and a number of point targets were very effectively put out of action by use of air power. Besides this, the force and performance ratios of the PAF and IAF actually deterred Pakistan from bringing its air force to support its army under attack by the IAF.

From the experience gathered in our wars, as well as from the wars fought in the last couple of decades, it is very apparent that air power has a crucial role to play. Before proceeding further, it would be prudent to understand the characteristics of future conflicts, and from this, define the role that the IAF as a future aerospace power, has to play.

CHARACTERISTICS OF FUTURE CONFLICTS

Future conflicts will require a high level of pre-emptive diplomacy, joint planning, surgical and precise operations, and active support by the media as well as the local populace. Large-scale wars are very unlikely, and we can expect short duration, limited conflicts; limited in terms of time, forces used, objectives and geographical extent. We can rest assured that international pressure and the threat of sanctions will terminate conflicts in a reasonably short time frame. Since time is limited in such clashes, it is essential that we act fast, well before the international community steps in to stop the war. Besides, the ever-increasing media awareness and access to remote areas in the shortest possible time due to modern technology, has put added pressure on the military for transparency in their operations. Globalization also has made nations more interdependent. It has ensured that conflicts, especially those with a military dimension, will impact even those countries that are not directly involved. In addition, economic compulsions have now exposed industries, civilian establishments and other targets of strategic value to the mercy of destruction by a determined enemy. Collateral damage can change the sentiment of the world, thus affecting the popular support of the masses.

Given the changing environment, the IAF of today will have to adapt itself to the needs of a different tomorrow. While the focus of our nation is still Pak-centric and centred on our borders, this will need to change to encompass our newly-defined and extended strategic borders. A degree of status quo exists on the borders, which are mainly brought about by terrain imperatives. This is unlikely to undergo much change, and we are already well prepared to meet any tactical contingencies that may arise in these areas. We should, therefore, re-orientate our strategies to cater to future conflicts based on our perceived threats to our strategic interests. Aerospace power can provide us with all the necessary tools to deter/conduct operations in the future.

ROLE OF AEROSPACE POWER

Today, with the availability of very accurate air-launched weapons and improved Intelligence, it can be expected that there will be precise targeting with minimal collateral damage. The requirement of speed, accuracy and lethality are the hallmarks of aerospace power. Apart from the ability to act quickly, aerospace power is ubiquitous and has the reach to strike deep and over a wide range of targets in a large geographical area. Aerospace power permits pre-emption and coercion and is a prime instrument for undertaking these tasks. Coercion requires political will, for example, enforcing no-fly zones. As regards the pre-emptive option, it will pay rich dividends, and should be exercised to exploit the existing conventional asymmetry available with us.

There is no pre-requisite to concentrate mass as in the earlier days, which allowed the opposition time to plan a defence that in turn resulted in a linear and sequential battle. Technology now permits parallel warfare, which allows simultaneously hitting of a number of targets in a well-orchestrated manner across the length and breadth of the country. The aim would be to disrupt/dislocate the enemy's centres of gravity. The targets could include leadership, command and control centres, civilian or military targets, etc. The Gulf War of 1990 presented a model script of the application of such a concept. Against this backdrop, it can be seen that aerospace power has truly come of age since the 1990s and has played a very dominant role in contributing to victory in the wars fought ever since. Therefore, the deterrence value, lethality, cost-effectiveness, time sensitivity, and inherent flexibility are characteristics of aerospace power. As such, these characteristics are best suited for playing a dominant and decisive role in future conflicts. What therefore are the implications for the IAF in the changing security environment of today?

PHILOSOPHY OF AIR OPERATIONS

Our strategy for air operations will necessarily flow from our military strategy. We strongly subscribe to the requirement for joint operations. This would translate to joint planning and execution at every possible level. This would automatically result in synergised joint operations. As far as the Air Force is concerned, we are fully geared for meeting the requirements of a 'cold start'. We have already drawn up our plans for this type of operations and have successfully put them to test in recent exercises. We have earmarked certain fighter squadrons as Core Sqns'. These squadrons are maintained at a readiness state that permits them to go into operation at a few hours' notice. Our war-orders and war-plans have been amended to cater to rapid induction and employment of these forces. Of course, we are aware that a lot depends upon whether we have the political will to take the decision to launch operations first. Nevertheless, we are training for such a requirement.

FUTURE PATH FOR THE IAF

Visions and Net-centric Warfare (NCW)

Aerospace power is synonymous with the air force. Getting down to specifics, first and foremost, is that the IAF has a vision that is linked to the vision of the country as a whole. As India grows as an economic power, it is inevitable that the Air Force will grow along with it. We believe that warfare is gradually moving into another dimension and that is space. So our Air Force's vision is to get into space. We are already using space for communications, reconnaissance and many other things. Everyone is talking about network-centric warfare. The future war is going to be lethal and fast paced. This requires faster decision making and faster implementation of decisions. Network-centric warfare (NCW) envisages the integration of information from all sensors and making it available as required and whenever required. This will provide a very high level of situational awareness, which is an essential ingredient while prosecuting a war. NCW functions at the operational level, but affects the strategic level as well.

Exploitation of Space

Space-based capabilities have perhaps had the most profound effect on airpower. It has enabled unprecedented compression of 'sensor-to-shooter' time. This allows 'time-sensitive targeting' almost anywhere on the globe. Exploitation of space, besides enhancing safety in air operations, exponentially adds to the speed, reach and flexibility of air power. Integration of the space dimension into air operations is essential for the IAF to attain strategic capability.

If space power needs to be exploited we must have a dedicated organization at the earliest to plan, steer and execute tasks to promote military applications. Whilst this organization must have representation from the three Services and scientists, we believe that this command must logically lie with the Air Force. Air power and space power need to be meshed into one as Aero Space Power. The IAF, therefore, strongly subscribes to the formation of a Space Command to exploit the military usage of space.

Presently, our (IAF) usage of space-based assets is restricted to gathering of strategic Intelligence, communications, weather, and for navigational assistance (GPS). With the introduction of cruise missiles (BrahMos), the entire operations would be fairly dependent on space-based assets. The operations would involve gathering Intelligence, ascertaining target locations, command and control of the weapon system, weather assessments, launches, enroute navigation, precision attacks and damage assessment.

Acquisition of Improved Sensors and Data Links

The IAF is in the process of looking at a data-link project to network all the airborne platforms and sensors with the ground sensors. The air defence network is being strengthened with modern sensors and weapon systems that include the AWACS, Aerostats and Air Defence missiles. All these force multipliers would substantially increase the potency, capability and reach of the Indian Air Force in the coming years.

FORCE STRUCTURING OF THE AIR FORCE

Need to Maintain Numbers

The IAF's force requirement is structured to meet two possible contingencies. The first contingency caters for a full conflict with Pakistan and a dissuasive posture against China. The second contingency is of simultaneous conflict with Pakistan and China, with a capability to hold Pakistan and defend against China. Whilst there is general talk of downsizing and modernization, the Air Force still needs the numbers.

The number of fighter squadrons has been gradually declining due to obsolescence and accidents over the past few years. To address this impending shortfall in the force level, the IAF has proposed to acquire an additional 126 medium multi-role combat aircraft (MMRCA). The aircraft that fits the bill for our requirement is the Mirage 2000 Mk II, F-16, Gripen and MiG-29 M2. We are looking at a Transfer of Technology (ToT) clause and sharing of software source code.

As a long-term strategy, we are planning to reduce the type of fighter aircraft in our inventory to three to four types. These would be long-range/heavy-weight fighters, medium range/medium weight multi-role fighters and lightweight low-cost fighter aircraft. In the first category, the IAF has already procured the SU-30, and in the third category the indigenous LCA would be acquired. Thus, the 126 fighter aircraft we are planning to procure need to be in the medium range/medium weight and multi-role category.

Upgrades

To obviate the need for purchasing expensive hardware, we have also gone in for the low-cost option of upgrading our existing aircraft. Upgradation of the MiG-21, MiG-27 and Jaguar aircraft is underway while the MiG-29 upgrade is in the pipeline.

Transport Aircraft

Our present fleet consists mainly of AN-32s and HS-748 ac in the below 5-ton payload class, and the IL-76 in the 40-ton class. Thus, there is clearly a gap in the aircraft capability between 5 ton and 40 ton payloads. Our requirement is 45 aircraft in this class. HAL is exploring the possibility of joint production of a transport aircraft of the 15-20 ton payload capacities. We need to increase our strategic lift capability to cater for out-of-area contingencies (OOAC) as well as relief during natural calamities.

Flight Refueller Aircraft

In our drive to enhance the reach of our aircraft, the IAF has acquired six aerial refuellers. We have since utilized these aerial refuellers to stage our fighter aircraft to Alaska, South Africa and France. These aircraft can also double up as cargo planes thereby enhancing our strategic lift capability. Our plans envisage that our future acquisitions of fighter, helicopter and transport aircraft will all be capable of being aerially refuelled. We have immediate plans of acquiring six additional flight refuelling aircraft. These aerial refuellers have given us global reach and a choice of options.

Helicopters

The IAF is processing a case for procurement of 80 Med Lift Helicopters. With induction of these helicopters, the IAF will be able to meet all the tasks as well as support UN peacekeeping operations. Acquisition of these additional MLH is in keeping with the overall plan for enhancement of the "strategic reach" of the IAF.

Indigenous Development

We are conscious of the undisputed need to be self-sufficient and therefore the requirement of promoting indigenous development. Despite slippages in the LCA programme, it is hoped that we would be able to operationalise two squadrons by the end of the 11th Plan. On the indigenous front, the IAF fully supports the involvement of the public and private sectors in these endeavours. However, there is a pressing need to adhere to time frames, especially for aviation-related technology, lest we face obsolescence at the time of induction itself. In this regard, we would like to see time-bound and quality systems being produced, which will interest buyers even in the international market.

RECENT ACHIEVEMENTS

Before concluding, I would like to briefly highlight some of the IAF's achievements in the past year.

Relief operations. During a number of occasions in aid to civil authorities, the IAF, since the tsunami disaster, has airlifted over 2,300 tons of material and 55,000 passengers. This has been unprecedented.

International exercises. The IAF has of late successfully trained with the air forces of the USA, France, Singapore and South Africa. From these exercises in which our air warriors displayed great professionalism, we were able to gain valuable operational lessons and experience.

UN Peacekeeping Operations. The IAF is currently manning three UN Peacekeeping Operations, two in Congo, and one in Sudan. The performance of the contingents has earned the nation accolades in the international arena.

CONCLUSION

The strength and credibility of the IAF today is a powerful deterrent to any hostile design. In order not only to maintain but also improve this capability, the modernization drive that we are undertaking is essential. With the induction and operationalisation of all the stated procurements, the IAF would be in a far better position to deal with the entire spectrum of threats, as also look after our extended strategic boundaries. Presently, we have the capability to deal with limited out-of-area contingencies. With exploitation of space-based resources, we would enhance our operational capability whilst simultaneously increasing our deterrent value.

We are currently focusing on training and development of human resources, as we are fully aware that it is the man behind the machine who will ultimately dictate our performance in any operation. Our endeavour is to improve the teeth-to-tail ratio, and in this regard, we are looking at measures to increase productivity and cost consciousness.

Finally, I can say with a great sense of satisfaction and due humility that each time the Indian Air Force was entrusted with a responsibility, it has delivered—whatever the odds. These tasks of responsibility have been achieved due to professionalism of the highest order, dedication to duty, and 'esprit-de-corps' amongst the Air Warriors.

Jai Hind

9

The Maritime Dimension of National Security

Admiral Arun Prakash,
PVSM, AVSM, VrC, VSM, ADC,
Chief of the Naval Staff

Introduction

I am indeed privileged to be present here today to deliver this year's General B.C. Joshi Memorial Lecture, which has been arranged by Pune University to mark this distinguished soldier's tenth death anniversary. Those who had the privilege of knowing General Joshi or serving under him are well aware that he was a far-sighted person, and one of his fondest visions was to ensure the spread of learning at all levels of the Indian Army. He was particularly keen that army officers should spend time in academic institutions, and had, therefore, established a unique and rather close relationship with academia, particularly with Pune University.

Gen. Joshi was instrumental in setting up the Chhatrapati Shivaji Chair in Policy Studies at this University, with the aim of encouraging research in national security issues. I think this was the first such chair instituted in India and, by a coincidence, just last month, I happened to inaugurate a Chair in Maritime Studies at the Calicut University. I feel that in a sense, the Navy is just walking down a trail pioneered by Gen. Joshi.

During his brief, but eventful tenure as the head of the world's third largest Army, General Joshi demonstrated all the attributes that the rank-and-file of the Armed Forces expect from a chief, but rarely find. He had a clear vision of where the army was going, and what he wanted for it. He was quick in decision-making because he had the ability to make rapid assessments. And above all, he had that one quality which soldiers long to see in their leaders: he was firm in his resolve and willing to stand up for the interests of the Service that he headed.

Just a month after he took over as Chief in August 1993, he addressed the officers in the College of Combat in Mhow. I happened to be undergoing a course there and recall sitting spell-bound while Gen. Joshi spoke for almost two hours ad lib without notes. In a speech of breath-taking scope and depth, the General explained in detail how he expected the Indian army to conduct itself in operations, from platoon, battalion, brigade and division levels right up to Corps and Armies. All of us present that morning knew that we had been listening to a brilliant soldier and an outstanding leader.

The General is today remembered with great regard for the substantive contributions he made in the field of education for children of army personnel. He was instrumental in setting up a number of centres of excellence of which the Army Institute of Technology here in Pune and the Army Hotel Management Institute in Bangalore are just two prime examples. Several similar institutions all over India are providing quality education to Army personnel.

While addressing the All-India Vice-Chancellor's Conference at Pune University on 13 November 1994, barely five days before he passed away, he had stated, "The next century will be India's century. This is not merely wishful thinking or building castles in the air, but the considered opinion of a soldier who has studied events and developments carefully." As India marches ahead into the 21st century, Gen. Joshi's words are proving to be prophetic indeed, and stand as testimony to this fine soldier's vision.

As I mentioned earlier, this happens to be the second occasion on which a university has invited me in my three months as Naval Chief. To my mind, this is a welcome sign, because "War", it has been said, "is too serious a business to be left to the Generals." In developed countries, almost all research in the field of national security is carried out in think tanks and institutions of higher learning, with the participation of academics as well as retired and serving Armed Forces officers. A similar trend is emerging in India too, and one finds that industrial houses and universities are willing to invest intellectual as well as financial resources in researching national security issues. The national security matrix today encompasses subjects ranging from the economy to the environment and from weapons to water. While this trend is indeed welcome, we as a nation do have a somewhat flawed perception of national security.

Our Flawed Security Perception

Such is our preoccupation with the politics of the day that, sadly, national security matters generally get relegated to the background. Attention on such issues tends to get focused only during periods of crisis, and the minute it is resolved, the nation seems to lose interest. There can be no doubt that the fundamental quest of our nation-state should be to provide a better quality of life for its teeming millions. However, the argument between guns and butter is not simply a zero sum game. If the past fifty-seven years have shown us anything, it is that you just cannot have development for your people unless you create a secure environment for the country. And a secure environment will be achieved only when it is clear to everyone in the neighbourhood that you are a strong, confident nation with a surplus of security assets and the resolute will to act in your national interest.

It would not be an exaggeration to state that our detached attitude towards national security (which includes Intelligence) has been the reason for the imposition of various conflicts on India by our neighbours from the invasion of Kashmir in 1947 to the occupation of the Kargil heights in 1999.

In my view, there are two major shortcomings in our system, which have a bearing on this state of affairs. The **first of these is our ambivalent attitude to national security and defence expenditure.** Every few years we tend to agonise over questions like: is there a threat to our national security or not? Do we need to commit funds to the Armed Forces on a long-term, or not? This attitude has led to fluctuating budgets and uncertainty in the force planning process. To compound the problem there is a total mismatch between the life of the defence budget, which is about 9-10 months and our decision-making process, which takes a minimum of 2-3 years. It should surprise no one that year after year, we are unable to expend the money voted for defence by Parliament. The present system of defence acquisition is guaranteed to ensure this.

This brings me to the **second factor; a strategic vision, or rather, the lack of it**. The question whether we as a nation and a cultural entity have lacked a tradition of strategic thinking and planning has been discussed often in recent times. While this debate may go on, the fact remains that for a variety of reasons, at present, our system does not take a long-term view of national security and this is why we often tend to react in a knee-jerk and uncoordinated manner to emerging threats and realities.

Every Indian citizen is a stakeholder in the nation's security. It is therefore necessary for not just the political establishment, but also for the media, the bureaucracy, and the academia to engage in a meaningful discourse on substantive issues. This would not only provide focus and a sense of direction to such debate, but would also remove the perception that India is a soft state.

If indifference to security issues is a national malaise, I must confess that disinterest in maritime security issues is a tendency, which is of equal concern. I therefore welcome this opportunity to speak to an audience such as this, specifically regarding the maritime dimension of national security. It is said that those who do not learn from history are condemned to live through it again. So with this in mind, let us delve a little into our maritime past.

The Indian Ocean and India's Maritime Past

"He who rules on the sea will shortly rule on the land also", was the advice given by the 16th century Ottoman Admiral Khaireddin Pasha (a.k.a. Barbarosa) to his Sultan Suleiman "the Magnificent" of Turkey. The history of no country illustrates this principle better than that of India. A majority of the invasions of India were from the landward side. But such invasions and conquests either led to transient political changes or to the foundation of new dynasties, which in a very short time were absorbed by the resilient fabric of India's culture, and became Indian. In fact, it may truly be said that India never lost her independence till she lost the command of the seas.

In ancient India, while the West Coast mainly witnessed commercial activity, the eastern waters were used as a medium for establishing longer lasting relationships. The deep cultural linkages of the subcontinent that are still very much in evidence with Myanmar, the Malayan peninsula, the islands of Sumatra, Java, and Bali in Indonesia, and with Thailand, Laos and Cambodia, stand witness to this.

The prowess at sea shown by the Mauryan dynasty, to which Emperor Ashoka belonged, was followed by maritime forays of the Pallava and Chola dynasties that set-up surrogate empires in South-east Asia. Indian seamen of that time were also at the forefront of development in seamanship and navigation and the invention of the magnetic compass or *"Matsya Yantra"* as it was then called, is ascribed to Indian navigators in ancient Egyptian texts.

I bring up these facts before this audience because most Indians, much less foreigners, are unaware that they are heirs to a rich maritime heritage, that their ancient forbears knew the seas well and used them for commercial, political and cultural purposes. Hence, we are neither strangers to the sea, nor interlopers in the Indian Ocean.

Till the beginning of the 16th century, because of the vast size of India and the insulation that Indian maritime power provided, oceanic problems had not really intruded into the history of the mainland. In fact, till the arrival of the Portuguese at Calicut in 1498, no naval power had appeared on Indian waters. The arrival of Vasco da Gama changed all that. From that time onwards till today, the powers that dominated the oceans have also dominated India.

The glory of the Mughal Empire on land could not hide its bankruptcy at sea. The Mughals, with their Central Asian tradition had, unfortunately, no recognition of the importance of the sea. The result was that during the two centuries of the Mughal Empire, not only did the Indian Ocean fall entirely under alien control, but simultaneously, the foundation was being laid by others for a more complete subjugation of India than any land power at any time could have conceived.

The decline of India's sea power by the 14th century in the Mughal era was to a large extent responsible for the success of the European adventurers who began to arrive on our shores in the next century. The Portuguese came first, followed by the Dutch, British and the French.

They came in search of spices, but stayed on to rule this land. The importance of the sea was realized by Indian rulers only when it was too late. In fact, apart from a few visionaries like Kunjali Marrakar and Kanhoji Angre, the Indian maritime scene was bereft of both the intellect and the will to use the seas to our advantage.

With Robert Clive's victory at the Battle of Plassey in June 1757, the Indian province of Bengal fell to the British. The thin end of the wedge was in position, and this date is commonly accepted as the beginning of Britain's 190-year rule of India. Commenting upon this historic event, Admiral Mahan in his seminal work, *"Influence of Sea Power on History"*, remarks, *"...It may be said that the foundation thus laid could never have been built upon, had the English nation not controlled the sea. The conditions in India were such that Europeans of nerve and shrewdness, dividing that they may conquer, and making judicious alliances, were able to hold their own against overwhelming odds."*

That our country has been prey to centuries of invasion and conquest, and that final domination by an alien power resulted not by overland invasion but by an onslaught across the seas is a fact that should be indelibly engraved in the mind of every Indian. It should also form the foundation and underpinning for our maritime thought. The USA succeeded Britain as the world's pre-eminent maritime power in the mid-20th century and remains so to this day. It is as a direct consequence of this attribute, that the USA is also the pre-eminent power in the world today.

Mackinder and the Heartland Theory

While most of us look at history as a record of inevitable events in human affairs, there are those who study it against the backdrop of *realpolitik* and look for cause and effect. One such person was Sir Halford Mackinder, a great scholar of political geography.

Examining the status of sea power in a geo-political context, Mackinder postulated the view that world history was a cyclic struggle between land-based and sea-based powers. He cited the example of Europe, where until AD 1500 AD, East European land powers from the European "heartland" had dominated the continent. However, the period from AD 1500-1900, which he termed as the Columbian era, witnessed the rise of "rimland" maritime powers like Britain, Spain, Holland and Portugal, because they exploited the mobility provided by the sea to give them an advantage over their territorial adversaries.

What Mackinder foresaw in 1904 was that the traditional advantage of mobility enjoyed by sea power was now being met in equal measure by mobility on land. The internal combustion engine, and the consequent development of the road and railway systems, had wrought this significant change. In 1919, he articulated the famous dictum that Eastern Europe was the key to the Heartland of Eurasia, which in turn commanded the World-Island. The power, which ruled the World-Island, ruled the World. It was this thesis that made Hitler roll his Panzers into Soviet Russia in 1941 in a desperate bid to gain control of the Heartland, prior to his intended conquest of the world.

Mackinder warned that the great continental powers in the heartland, with their hinterland full of resources, were ascendant. They would soon develop their capabilities to a point where they would break the barriers imposed upon them by the rimland and surge out to the sea. In a sense, he foresaw the demise of Great Britain as a world power half a century before it actually happened, and till the late 1980s, when the erstwhile Soviet Union and the USA were the two superpowers, it was fashionable to quote Mackinder's prophesies.

However, what people failed to notice was the fact that the USA, which was by then of course a continental power, had also developed into a maritime power, whereas the Soviet Union remained essentially a continental power. One analysis sums up the developments of the past 25 years as follows: *"The United States actually encircled the Soviet Union under the famous Doctrine of Containment, principally using its maritime power, that is carriers and nuclear submarines, as the vehicle for this effort. By enlisting the rimland countries against the Soviets, by using central Europe as a bridgehead, Great Britain as an advanced air base, and Canada and the USA as resource bases for material and manpower, they denied the Soviets access to the sea and ultimately won the Cold War."*

Some may dismiss this as a facile and simplistic explanation of a momentous historical event beset with complex geo-strategic and economic nuances. However, an analysis of the last few centuries does throw up the fact that continental powers have historically fared poorly against maritime powers. The reason is simple. The seas offered unrestricted space for movement and access, which when exploited, led to immense economic gains. This, in turn, gave countries the ability to finance a large military, including a powerful navy, and thus the cycle goes on.

Today, the USA, the dominant maritime power, is also the sole superpower. Russia, whose status as a first-class power is questionable, now has to vie with the USA for influence over Central Asia, which is an enormous repository of fossil fuel. Geopolitics is however an uncertain science, and whether the future will mirror the past remains to be seen.

Let me next come to India's stake in the seas that surround us, or what is termed as, our maritime interests.

India's Maritime Interest

Pandit Jawaharlal Nehru had once stated: "We cannot afford to be weak at sea. History has shown that whatever power controls the Indian Ocean, has in the instance, India's sea borne trade at her mercy, and the second, India's very independence itself". India's national objectives lie in ensuring a secure and stable environment, which will permit the economic development and social uplift of its masses, so that the country can ultimately take its rightful place in the international comity of nations. Within this overall objective, our prime maritime interest is to ensure national security and provide insulation from external interference, so that the vital tasks of fostering economic growth, and undertaking developmental activities, can take place in a secure environment. In this context, national security encompasses certain economic factors in the maritime domain, which I would like to mention here.

Overseas trade. Reforms in the past decade have resumed in a liberalized Indian economy, integrated with and increasingly interdependent on other world economies. India is now projected to become the fourth largest economy in the world by 2020, after China, Japan and the USA. Our foreign trade of approximately US$ 95 billion accounts for about a fifth of our GDP. Of this trade, 77 per cent by value and over 90 per cent by volume is carried by sea. The tremendous scope for further growth can be imagined when we consider that our share of the world trade is only 0.62 per cent.

Energy needs. The critical importance of a continuous and assured supply of energy resources such as oil, natural gas and coal for a growing economy like ours cannot be underestimated. According to current projections, with steady industrial growth India would, in a few years, become the world's largest consumer of petroleum products. With limited domestic production, the import element, currently at 60 to 70 per cent is going to steadily keep rising. While talk of pipelines continues, we may safely assume that ships will carry much of these energy imports across vulnerable sea-lanes.

Undersea resources. Another facet of the ocean, which presents the prospect of wealth and prosperity, and yet contains the seeds of future conflict, is undersea resources. Our offshore hydrocarbons represent a vital asset as well as a maritime liability. The average depth of the Indian Ocean is about 4 km and that is the distance, which separates us from a treasure house of rare minerals, in the form of poly-metallic nodules awaiting exploitation on the ocean bed. India has a mineral-rich EEZ currently extending over 2.2 m sq km, and the successful exploitation of these could lift us from economic backwardness.

Merchant fleet and ports. India's merchant navy is small for our needs, and size. Relatively speaking, it constitutes a little over one percent of the world shipping tonnage, and our ships are able to carry only about a third of our own foreign trade. However, in absolute terms, India's growing fleet of over 600 ships is quite large, and operates out of 12 major and 184 minor ports. The security of these ports, our merchant ships and the sea-lanes that they play on represent vital maritime interests for us.

Having seen the geo-strategic importance of the seas, let me highlight a few important attributes of maritime power.

Attributes of Maritime Power

In 1905, when the Royal Navy was seriously contemplating drastic cuts in the size of the fleet as an economy measure, the British Foreign Office complained bitterly. *"If the number of ships is to be reduced to an extent that the Royal Navy will not be able to give the foreign policy of this country such support as is expected by the Foreign Office, we can only conclude that the vital interests of the country are being sacrificed in the interest of false economy."*

This was, of course, a statement made in the heyday of what was known as "gunboat diplomacy". But today, more than ever, navies form a potent instrument of state policy provided that wisdom and imagination exist to wield this instrument in furtherance of national interests. The oceans remain the *"common heritage"* of mankind and freedom of navigation on the high seas is a fundamental principle of maritime law. Unlike every inch of land on the continents, the seas in their natural state are free of political control.

Seventy percent of the Earth's surface is covered by the sea and over two-thirds of the world's population lives within 100 miles of it. Over 150 of the 185 member-states of the UN are coastal states. Since the 1970s, they have all extended their jurisdiction out to sea—in many cases, by as much as 200 m and some beyond that. Most human maritime activity is confined to within 100 nm of the coastal zones. This means that a very large proposition of the world's economic, industrial and political activity is carried out in this swath of land and sea extending about 300 nm. This is often referred to as the littoral and that is where the navies of the major maritime powers are focusing today. It is noteworthy that in all of the recent major conflicts—Kosovo, Afghanistan and Iraq—the major intervention by coalition forces has not been overland but from the littoral. The intervention came through naval aviation through launch of cruise missiles by ships or submarines or by landing of marine expeditionary units.

All applications of sea power flow from the fact that the sea is the greatest of highways. It is much easier to move a ton of commodities, oil, or military hardware by water than by land or air. Contrary to Mackinder's beliefs, today, the USA finds it cheaper to ship semi-conductors from Malaysia or cars from Japan than to carry the same items from its east coast to the west coast by land or rail. The fundamental quest in maritime warfare, therefore, has always been to secure the free use of the sea highway for oneself and to deny it to the enemy because the economic lifelines of nations run across the seas.

It is in this context that I would like you to look at certain distinctive attributes of maritime power, which make it unique and invest it with the potential to act as the handmaiden of state power or diplomacy without even leaving a footprint in its wake.

- **Access.** The sea covers over two-thirds of the globe and this allows maritime forces to exploit the oceans for their unhindered deployment in areas of interest or threat. International law provides free and legal access for ships up to the territorial waters of nations, and also allows the right of what is called **innocent passage** for traversing these waters. As Op Enduring Freedom showed recently, even landlocked states can become accessible from the sea provided intervening coastal states co-operate. At the same time, the medium of the sea provides the contiguity to convert distant nations into neighbours—friendly or otherwise. The UK and Argentina, separated by 2,000 miles fought a war through the medium of the sea in 1982.
- **Versatility.** Warships can easily change their posture, undertake several tasks concurrently, and be rapidly available for re-tasking. Warships at readiness are always manned and provisioned to sail at short notice for ops commitments. Individual ships of frigate size and above will always have capabilities in all three dimensions, and warships can be formed into task forces, which provide a mutually supportive combination of offensive and defensive capabilities.
- **Sustained reach.** Maritime forces have integral logistic support including re-fuelling, repair and medical facilities. The range and endurance that these provide gives maritime the sustained reach, which is the ability to operate at a considerable distance from shore support.

Roles

Against this backdrop, can be seen that maritime forces have an application in a wide range of operations at sea, extending from nuclear conflict or high-intensity war fighting at one end of the spectrum, to humanitarian relief and stable peace at the other. This range of operations can be broken down into four compartments or types of roles, which may, in general terms, be described as **military, diplomatic, constabulary** and **benign**:

- **Military.** Where combat is used or threatened, or which pre-supposes a combat capability. This includes the application of maritime power at sea, and also from the sea in both offensive operations conducted against enemy forces and defensive operations conducted to protect friendly forces and maritime trade. In our context, Sea Control, Sea Denial, Blockade and LIMO are few examples of this role.

- **Diplomatic.** Military force at sea contributes to what is traditionally known as Naval Diplomacy. It is the use of maritime forces as a diplomatic instrument in support of political objectives and foreign policy. It assumes the availability of force to backup and support diplomatic efforts at various levels.
- **Constabulary.** Where forces are employed to enforce law, or some regime established by international mandate. In this role, violence is used only in self-defence or as a measure of last resort in execution of the task. In the Indian context, some of these tasks have been assigned to the Coast Guard.
- **Benign.** Tasks such as humanitarian aid, disaster relief, SAR, salvage assistance or hydrography are classified under the heading of "benign". Such tasks may require the specific capabilities and specialist knowledge of our forces in an emergency. Violence has no part to play in its execution, nor is the potential to apply force a pre-requisite.

In general, the Indian Navy can be the catalyst for peace tranquillity and stability in the Indian Ocean Region, across a wide range of conditions and circumstances that one can envisage in peacetime. The imaginative use of the navy can achieve this in more ways than one. It can be used to engage other maritime nations and extend our hand of friendship and co-operation. Its robust presence in a particular area or region could contribute to stability and ensure peace. Lastly, it can act as a strong deterrent with the ability to prevent conflict, or to respond, should it become necessary.

Let us then move on to the challenges of the future, and how these will shape the maritime strategy for India in the foreseeable future.

The Strategic Context

It is an accepted tenet of international relations that nations do not have permanent friends or permanent enemies, but only permanent interests. The order of battle of the IN is not configured on the basis of perceived threats to our security, but on the basis of capabilities existing in our neighbourhood and the likelihood of emergent challenges. The underlying premise is that if a capability exists, or is being developed by a country with which we share boundaries or interests, it could have a bearing on our security, should circumstances or intentions change over time.

Let me now briefly outline the future strategic context, and the likely challenges in the maritime context, as I see them at the present juncture.

The Security Scenario

To start with, our field of view extends from the Persian Gulf, down the East coast of Africa, and across to the Malacca Strait which contains the area of direct interest to us. Let us look at who are likely to be major players and what are the issues in this region? Certain international security trends can be discerned based on current form.

The USA will certainly remain the sole superpower for the foreseeable future. The EU, China, Japan, Russia and India are likely to be the other reckonable powers in the world. The USA will remain actively engaged in the Asia-Pacific region. Underpinning all her policies is the ever present and overriding need to have access to the oil fields and markets of this region, so that her own oil reserves remain intact, and her economy buoyant. The USA also has a requirement to fulfil security obligations to countries like Japan, Taiwan and South Korea. A concomitant requirement is to contain or engage China's growing power. It is interesting to see a gradual transition of US security policies to suit its national interests, from a Cold War posture to its present stance.

Therefore, as the Prime Minister of India stated last week, *"For India, engaging the USA is a necessity."* The Indian Navy has been a prime instrument for this engagement and many here may not know that the first military engagements with the USA after the end of the Cold War were in the form of naval exercises that were first carried out in 1991. The reason why the Navy was the forerunner in breaking the ice with the USA was of course the fact that ships and fleets operate beyond the horizon, and leave no "footprints" on land. Since then, we have progressed to the stage of advanced-level exercises where even their nuclear submarines participate regularly.

The fountainhead of terrorism and focal point of nuclear and missile technology proliferation is located right next doors to us. Defying predictions, our neighbour, Pakistan, has made a remarkable economic recovery, and by playing its cards right, derived maximum advantage in the post-9/11 scenario. From recent experience, it has learnt a cautionary lesson about maritime security, and with substantive help from China, and perhaps the USA, it is in the process of adding hardware to its navy. China is also constructing a strategic alternative to Karachi port in Gwadar on the Makaran coast. Gwadar sits astride the exit to the Persian Gulf, and an eventual Chinese naval presence there would be of concern to us.

China's defence spending today runs to about five times ours. It is taking full advantage of the prevailing tranquillity, and her buoyant economy, to modernize its armed forces. Even if we discount any expansionist designs, China's desire to safeguard its growing energy dependence on the Gulf will see it building up the PLA (Navy). While major warships, diesel submarines, and long-range strike aircraft are being sourced from Russia, its own industry is producing nuclear submarines and long-range ballistic missiles. China is intensely engaged with almost all countries in our immediate neighbourhood. It has in place, agreements for supply of military hardware to these countries, and maintains very cordial relations with them, which is more than what we can see for ourselves.

It is an unfortunate fact that for various reasons, our relations with countries all round are under a degree of strain. In my opinion, we have for far too long neglected our smaller neighbours and demanded "reciprocity", when our relative size, economy, and above all tenets of good-neighbourliness actually suggested "generosity".

Trade inter-dependence within the region is already a reality and will grow even further. As a result of the economic boom, the Asia-Pacific region's share of world energy consumption will continue to rise and the energy security will assume progressively greater significance. India's own oil consumption is expected to rise to 150 million tons by 2020, with the country likely to be the world's single largest importer of oil by 2050. Consequently, stakes in the security of the vital sea lanes and the pressure on countries to cooperate in the maritime domain will grow enormously. Any challenge to the free flow of oil, which can be interrupted by a host of state and non-state agencies, can lead to a major conflict, which can have profound effects on the world economy.

Terrorism will continue to unite and divide nations. Terrorist threats of transporting men and material (especially WMD) through sea routes will continue to drive multilateral security initiatives by the USA. Three of them—the International Ship and Port Security Code (ISPS Code), the Proliferation Security Initiative (PSI) and the Container Security Initiative (CSI)—are already in various stages of implementation. Once again, the maritime dimension is taking the lead in implementing these collective security measures.

Low-Intensity Maritime Operations involving political as well as criminal entities, will gain in importance. The Indian Navy and the Coast Guard have been engaged insecurity duties in the Palk Bay, along our maritime boundary with Sri Lanka, since the late Eighties. On the west coast too, the Navy has been conducting surveillance operations since 1993 consequent to the Bombay blasts. With the complete fencing of our western land borders, a resurgence of clandestine activity at sea can be anticipated.

The need to exploit marine resources and dependence on the sea for food, energy and minerals will grow exponentially. This will necessitate a quantum increase in our efforts to ensure the maritime security of littoral assets.

Conclusion

As I near the end of my talk, let me wind up by leaving some food for thought.

When I interact with my counterparts in other navies, especially some from the Western Hemisphere, the questions most frequently put to me are: What is the purpose of your large navy? Why are you buying or building ships and aircraft carriers? Why does your Maritime Doctrine talk of a sea-based nuclear deterrent?

From this line of questioning, it becomes obvious that the colonial mindset does linger on in some quarters. In the old days, it was understood that maintaining peace, law and order east of the Suez was the "white man's burden", and it still appears preposterous to some that a third world navy should presume to shoulder it. The best that can be done is to put across a balanced Indian perspective on such matters, and hope that one's interlocutor is convinced.

But what does one do when the same or similar reservations are often expressed by one's own compatriots? Essentially, sceptics say that all our security problems are concentrated in the north and east, so why spend money on a navy. Of late, defence expenditure is also being questioned in the context of peace talks and CBMS under discussion.

I would like to draw attention to the fact that historically, in international relations, a power imbalance in any region has always led to instability and eventually to war. In the Asia-Pacific region, there are a number of economic and military power centres, either existing or emerging, and the pre-eminent among these are China and India. It is in the nature of things that the stronger power will try to dominate and establish hegemony over the others.

In such a situation, unless a balance of power can be established, either the weaker power capitulates without a struggle, or there is a conflict. History has shown that appeasement only whets the appetite of totalitarian states. While we have no wish to dominate anyone, we need to ensure that nobody else is in a position to dictate terms to us either. And for this, it is essential to build and maintain a credible deterrent military capability, of which a strong navy is an essential ingredient.

With the global security environment now focused on the Asia-Pacific, the Indian Ocean Region has become critically important to many major powers. Today, the Asia-Pacific contains almost 4 billion of the world's over 6 billion people and accounts for 60 per cent of the world's GDP. By 2020, seven of the ten largest economies in the world will be in this region, making the 21st century truly the "Asia-Pacific century". While the region holds great economic potential, it also contains the seeds of conflict in several areas, and has lately become prey to the scourge of religious fundamentalism.

For India, the Asia-Pacific region holds immense promise for political, economic and military co-operation, and the key role that maritime forces can play makes the Indian Navy an important component of any national strategy designed for this region.

However, a capable navy is only one element of maritime power. A large merchant fleet, modern ports with good infrastructure and a vibrant, efficient and self-reliant shipbuilding industry along with its supporting technical infrastructure are some of the other vital ingredients of maritime power that we need to concentrate upon.

The key fact, however, lies in the populace having a maritime temperament and outlook. Indians, in general, need to acknowledge that if not a "maritime nation" (yet), we certainly are a nation dependant on the seas, and need to look more seawards than inwards. Such a realization is especially vital for people at what is called the decision-making or political level of security planning. Only then can we stake our claim to be a true maritime power.

Thank you very much for your attention.

Jai Hind

10

Examining the Concept of 'National Security'

George Fernandes,
Trade Unionist, Political Activist and Journalist

The late General Joshi, former Chief of Army staff and Army Commander here in Pune, was clearly a man of many parts and talents. He died seven years ago in harness—on November 18, 1994 and from what I can gather, he was endowed with a clear vision about the future of the Indian army as an institution. The role and relevance of the 'fauj' in the national security calculus, at a time when the global order was still adjusting to the end of the Cold War, and the challenge of internal security was becoming more complex and onerous in the Indian case, required astute attention by the armed forces.

The scourge of terrorism and the cross-border support abetting this malignancy was an issue that General Joshi was deeply cognizant of and he was instrumental in the resolution of the Hazratbal crisis. Subsequently it was at his behest that the Government of the day approved the creation of the RR—the Rashtriya Rifles. This Force has provided the requisite continuity in the LIC/IS grid and also allowed the Army to retain a strategic reserve for other-border variant continues to test our resolve and the attack on the Indian Parliament on December 13 last, is a case in point.

In addition to other initiatives, Bipin Joshi was also instrumental in the setting up of chairs of excellence to encourage Indian academia to study the myriad challenges the nation now faces and the Department of Defence here in Pune University is a direct beneficiary. I exhort the members of the academic and strategic community here in Pune to realize the vision that was outlined by General Joshi—and my only advice is do not settle for the average or the mediocre. Set a yardstick for yourselves that is 37 inches, so that in the near future, Pune is acknowledged both nationally and regionally—and I hope one day internationally—as a credible center for Defence Studies, whose excellence speaks for itself.

Mr. Chairman, allow me to now turn to the larger issue of national security and I will attempt to approach this subject in a slightly elliptical manner. Perhaps examining the concept of 'national security' per se offers a useful point of departure and from this general survey, we may be able to extrapolate to the specific Indian example. History is replete with instances of conquest and defeat, of war and bloodshed and it may not be invalid to suggest that the military component of history and the security of states is the dominant thread in the evolution of mankind. From the wooden club of yore to the nuclear tipped-missile of today, mankind and the collective structures they form have lived with their deepest insecurities of personal safety and security. Certain correspondences are inevitable and thus it is not without reason that the ancient Greek historian Thucydides noted that "States, like men, cannot be blamed for providing for their proper safety."

Human thought has cogitated at length about this primary aspect of survival and one can come across many such references embedded in the earliest civilizations of the world. India is an ancient civilization-state perhaps the only unbroken one that has evolved from one historical epoch to another without repudiating its past and I shall highlight some aspects of the earliest interpretative accounts of the concept of national security. Ideologically India has been wedded to the concepts of peace and non-violence on one hand, and equity and rectitude on the other. The latter concept is often referred to as 'dharma' in early Indian thought and allows me to dilate on this concept or value.

Dharma is applicable to individuals and institutions, and moves along the socio-political scale to encompass larger groups such as the family, the extended community/village and could be extrapolated to the nation-state in its modern sense. Thus, a relationship between states predicted upon a true adherence to the spirit of dharma, which steers national endeavour towards Shanti of equitable peace, to my mind, forms the conceptual bedrock of comprehensive security in an Indian matrix.

It must also be added here that for such security to be truly comprehensive, this adherence to the twin concepts of dharma and Shanti between states would need perforce to be complemented by a commitments towards the security of the individuals who constitute the said states. This internal dimension may not be within the purview of our current deliberations but the dharma or duty of a ruler also emphasizes this aspect. According to the Arthashastra of Kautilya (c. 4th century BC) a harmonious relationship between the ruler and the ruled or populate is mandatory and I quote from the text: "In the happiness of his subjects lies his (ruler's welfare). He shall not consider as good only that which pleases him but treat as beneficial to him whatever pleases his subjects."

In the commentary accompanying the Arthashastra, this is elucidated as: "The duty of the ruler to protect his subjects is, however, often expressed not in terms of raksana (protection) or palana (governance) but in terms of ensuring their yogaksema. This implies something more than mere protection of person and property. Yoga refers to the successful accomplishment of an object, while ksema refers to the peaceful, undisturbed enjoyment of that objects... yogaksema implies the idea of welfare, well-being, including the idea of prosperity, happiness and contentment."

Thus, truly comprehensive security must move harmoniously from the individual to the larger group coalescing in the nation-state. If yogaksema addresses the security within the state, the twin concepts of dharma and Shanti define the framework for such comprehensive security among states. Ancient Indian thought perceived the whole world as being one extended family—concept of vasudhaivakutumbakam—and situated human endeavor and aspiration within the larger canvas of nature and a macro cosmic order.

Here the correspondences with last 20th century anxieties about ecological balances and environmental protection in an interdependent world need little reiteration. In essence, there is a conceptual linkage between what constituted macro-security at that point in times the imperatives of state and ruler, with the dictates of micro-security the protection and well-being of the individual. And normatively, we find this core being retained consistently in the modern Indian sensibility.

However the modern security experiences post 1947 is a chequered history. A certain degree of idealism permeated the Indian posture in the early decades and the relevance of military preparedness and credibility in underpinning foreign policy was notable by its absence. Thus the first was for Kashmir in 1947-48 and the 1962 trauma with China ensued. More recently the 40th anniversary of this experience was recalled—and let me add without rancor or bitterness—the idea being to learn from this experience. I cannot claim to be a net surfer but I did see many residents of Pune contributing to this debate about 1962. What is evident in hindsight is that there was an inadequate awareness about military capabilities, and the inexorable linkage with the core national interest and integrity.

Many in this audience would be familiar with the Nehruvian paradigm of India's early decades and his vision of how India's interests could be best protected. Development and socio-economic progress was ostensibly prioritized in the first decades after independence but the inadequacies in the defence sector led to a grave imbalance in the Indian posture of the period. Basically defence and development were seen as being two different aspects of the collective Indian endeavor.

It is one of those ignored anomalies that notwithstanding the reality that India has a very complex security environment, free India allocated very modest resources to the defence sector. This hovered between 1.5 to 3.5 percent of the GDP. It is currently around 2.5 percent and has always been under 4 percent. There is good reason for this modest allocation towards defence. As an impoverished nation that has millions below the poverty line, the primary objective of the state is to improve the socio-economic conditions and opportunities for the masses and hence the priority on the development sectors. This division between defence and development is an abiding feature of the Indian system and many of you would have noted that the Indian budget classifies the defence expenditure as part of the Non-Plan expenditure, whereas the entire development allocation is part of the Plan expenditure.

But let me give you another perception from an equally distinguished Indian Ram Manohar Lohia—a great socialist leader and my political mentor. Translated from the Hindi, he used to often say that if the closed fist is analogous to the military capability of the state, then the arm that supports the fist is the collective of state and society. The synergism in the analogy between defence and development is evident and needs little reiteration. This has been my personal conviction, also and again, as many in this audience may be aware, the NDA government that Mr. Vajpayee heads had dwelt on this aspect the need for a credible defence profile and the linkage with the rest of the collective capability. This was reiterated as part of the election manifesto and the agenda for governance that was issued soon after the NDA was elected to office.

This assertion of the need for India to acquire a credible defence posture and capability should not be misconstrued as advocating belligerence or engaging in an arid arms race. That pattern of state response was a relief of the Cold War. The global strategic and security environment has changed considerably with the internment of bipolarity and the collapse of the former Soviet Union. There is little doubt the USA is the most pre-eminent power today—some describe it as the lone super-power, others as the hydro-power though the more piquant description may be that of the lonely super-power.

Be that as it may, there is a consensus today that national security cannot be perceived and pursued in the manner that it was during the Cold war decades. If security was an exclusive concept in the Cold War that focused only on the military dimension—that is the nuclear weapon and the missile—today it has become an inclusive concept. Paul Kennedy in his well-known book on the rise and fall of great powers has written about this far more cogently and in much greater depth. States have to harmonize their disparate capabilities and find the right degree of synergism, and, the primary attributes are the political, economic and military capabilities of a state and its human resource—or civil society. These basic attributes need to be buttressed by other strands such as intellectual and technological prowess, environmental resilience and ultimately—societal indicators. The era of globalization and free market enterprise is upon us and the anxiety that it may engulf the vulnerable is not unfounded. Trade and profit is the new mantra—within and among states and civil society. The stock market is the new totem but the fear that the gap between the haves and have-nots will keep growing is very real and the long-term security implications of such disparity are self-evident.

Thus India's primary strategic objective to my mind is the improvement of the socio-economic conditions and opportunities within a secular democratic framework for its one billion people. However while this vast human resource is the ultimate reservoir and asset in terms of national wealth and potential, the conditions for ensuring that the overall environment is conducive for such socio-economic growth has to come from a secure domestic and regional environment. In other words, to revert to the Lohia analogy—the fist can be only as strong and resilient as the arm and shoulder that supports it, and the latter can only be as secure and stable as the fist that protects it.

It is in this overall context that I would like to locate India's national security and the relevance of the military or defence capability. Prima facie, the territorial integrity and safety of the people is the sine quo non-for the existence of the defence infrastructure and this is a tenet of both international relations and political science. India is not alone in the prioritizations of such interests. Linked with this is the need for India to acquire a profile of quiet confidence devoid of any belligerence—that would allow it to exercise its autonomy and freedom—albeit in a responsible manner. While recognizing the contours of the inter-dependence that links the post-Cold War world together, and notwithstanding the many daunting tasks that challenge the mettle of Indian state and society—an intangible but essential objective would be to ensure that India, in its engagement with the international 'systemic'—or the global comity, is not subjected to any kind of anxiety or fear of intimidation—political, economic or military.

Within this matrix, both economic and defence capabilities on one hand, and politico-diplomatic relations on the other are equally important. But let me dwell on the defence/military aspects. At the macro level, the NDA as a government with Mr. Vaipayee at the helm deemed it necessary for India to conduct the nuclear tests of May 1998 and acquire a credible minimum deterrent. Given the prevailing global strategic environment and the manner, in which WMD capabilities were being used to vitiate our neighbourhood, we were convinced that India's security interests were best served by exercising the option that had been kept open for decades.

Many significant and seminal developments have punctuated the international system and India's bi-lateral relations over the last five years and Mr. Chairman, with your permission, I would like to dwell on one specific determinant the India-US relationship. As this audience is well aware, the end of the Cold War accorded an opportunity for both states to review a relationship that was till then described as 'estranged'. The Clinton years outlined the potential contours of this relationship and I may add that the Indian nuclear tests of May 1998 helped to clear the air as it were, about how India wished to pursue its national interest and the bi-lateral relationships attendant upon nurturing this core interest. The professionals on both sides—that is India and the USA—played a commendable role in stabilizing the bi-lateral relationship that moved from 'estrangement' to 'engagement'. Subsequently, US President Mr. George Bush and our PM Atalji made it abundantly clear that the bi-lateral relationship would be accorded its own autonomy and not be predicated upon any other factor. I hope this will put to rest the incessant speculation and frenzied comment on both sides about the relevance of the 'other' in the India-US matrix. It is a matter of quite satisfaction that today—even as we meet here—the bi-lateral relationship between India and the USA is becoming more robust across the board.

The one event that has had a tectonic effect on US security consciousness and by extension on the global discourse is what is often referred to as "9-11"—the tragic events of September 11 last. Terrorism and the support this phenomenon receives from deviant regimes had a dramatic impact on the USA and brought to the fore Washington's determination to deal with this scourge. In the last year, India and the US have interacted at many levels from the highest political to the more regular meetings of officials to forge a common stance to address the cancer of terrorism and realize the spirit of UN Security Council resolution 1373. And as I have said often to my counterparts Donald Rumsfeld and Paul Wolfowitz, we in India have been dealing with the problem of terrorism, misplaced religious zealotry and deviant regime support to this malignancy almost since the birth of free India in 1947.

Now that the naked face of terrorism and what it implies has been unequivocally established in the post 9-11 context, there are many correspondences and convergence's as far as India and the USA are concerned. It will be a tribute to the professionalism and commitment of the various actors in this bi-lateral relationship when it realizes the potential it holds. Let me briefly enumerate what brings India and the USA together at this point in time and why we value our relationship with Washington. The nature of the asymmetry between our economic and military indicators needs little reiteration. America's GDP is more than 20 times that of India and its technological index is far ahead of what we make do with less than US $ 14 billion to manage India's myriad security challenges, while the USA I am told will soon reach the US $ 450 billion mark for its defence outlay.

But more than the glaring asymmetries; what brings us together is a shared empathy for abiding values. This is not a cliché. It is often said that India and the USA are the world's two largest democracies, and I agree that espousing mere rhetorical commitment to this characteristic is not enough to provide the bonding for the relationships. We need to increase the content of the economic and military relationship within the framework outlined by both sides and here in believe that while the trade and technology progress is modest by prevailing international Standards—it is headed in the right direction. The democratic nature apart—India and the USA are essentially techno-savvy—and if the recent Bill Gates visit and the insights about how much Indian brainpower contributed to Microsoft is any indicator-then it may yet be possible for India to leap-frog and catch up with the developed nations and improve the quality of life for its millions. I have often maintained that if China, South Korea and parts of ASEAN can do it why not India? We have to find the appropriate degree of collective determination and that intangible—national will—to redress the many inadequacies that stare us in the face.

On the security and strategic front, I am of the considered view that there are many correspondences for India and the USA. Post 9-11 we are both committed to dealing with the complex manifestations of state sponsored terrorism; we are cognizant of the threats posed by weapons of mass destruction and the need to manage this capability prudently and in keeping with the altered techno-strategic environment of the current times; and the need to sustain both regional and global security and stability. The ultimate ends or the objectives converge, though we may not transverse similar paths in the means adopted to arrive at specific goals. And yes, our perceptions may differ as for instance in how we perceive the current regimes in either Baghdad or Islamabad. But what is encouraging is the fact that we are now able to manage our differences in quiet consultation at the appropriate level without slipping into the kind of acrimonious public exchanges characteristic of the Cold War decades.

I am not suggesting that we completely forget the past. This is not advisable for it is a tenet of human nature that those who obliterate their past experience may be condemned to repeat it in the future. What we should strive for is to ensure that while the past is metaphorically part of the 'hard disk' on both sides, it is not allowed to 'corrupt' the future. In recent weeks, I have seen some references to the bitterness of bygone decades—for e.g. transcripts of tapes relating to exchanges between former US President Nixon and the redoubtable Mr. Henry Kissinger with other Asian leaders and some less than complimentary references to India. Let us put that aside—we in India need to quarantine 1971 and the USS Enterprise, while the USA may like to similarly bury the perception of India as a Soviet lackey and such like.

We should look at the positive side of this phase of our relationship and I remind my domestic interlocutors that whenever the US has taken a firm stand against us—or 'sanctioned' us—we have found the inner resolve to convert tribulation into triumph. The Indian determination to innovate in the computer field and come up with PARAM, or the remarkable Indian design of the APSOH sonar is a case in point.

It is in the military security field that I envisage considerable scope for arriving at consensual mutuality on both sides. The profile of the Indian military is modest in comparison to the technological quality and quantitative indicators of the US armed forces, yet in recent months we have interacted to mutual benefit. The land, air and maritime forces have exercised with each other and identified areas for further cooperation. Whether it is the Indian expertise in combating terrorism and low insurgency as evidenced in our College set-up in Mizoram, or the expertise acquired in UN Peace Keeping operations. India can bring some distinctive attributes to the table and benefit from access to US military technology and related industry.

The one domain that has immediate and tangible potential for cooperation is the naval-maritime one. Today the maritime focus of the world has shifted from the Atlantic-Pacific combine of the Cold War decades to the Pacific-Indian Ocean combine that straddles the oil rich Gulf through the Malacca Straits, to the Sea of Japan. Ensuring the safety and stability of the sea-lines of communication is a common strategic objective for all major powers. Piracy and the threat from non-state actors must be thwarted and the oceans and seas kept as safe and low-threat as they now are. India has been working towards this end with all like-minded states in the Indian Ocean littoral. More recently India has agreed to escort high-value US bottoms through the Indian Ocean in support of the US campaign against terrorism, and the high professionalism of the Indian Navy—and the Coast Guard have been acknowledged. What is germane is the recognition that India is a credible and stabilizing force in the maritime domain where it has established a reasonable 'presence in tandem with other navies.

This brings me Mr. Chairman, to the final point that I wish to elucidate—and I hope this will not be construed as a case of belaboring the obvious. Today, when the global community is adjusting to the post 9-11 ambiance, I aver that the security of states and civil society has become more indivisible and seamless than ever before. This is an existential reality. Individually we may take time to comprehend the import of this assertion but if there is a classification of states and civil society today, I know what it is NOT. It is not along the East-West ideological division of the Cold War, or the North-South chasm of economic indicators, or the contested fault-lines of the clash of civilizations. Today states and their ruling elite, to my mind, will be assessed in terms of how much they strengthen and advance the normative values of freedom, liberty, tolerance and equitable prosperity. On the other hand regimes and elites who subvert stability, degrade collective security and support the suppression of these normative values will be gradually isolated—both by their people and the global community. Thus state rectitude becomes an important index, and Mr. Chairman, I assert that this is India's distinctive characteristic. We have defied this value and endeavored to be consistent in both word and deed through the Cold War decades to the present times.

Allow me to make a slight digression here. Among the many

distinctive features that one associates with the values that underpin the Indian experience is the commitment to secularism. This commitment flows from the Constitution that the founding fathers gave unto India and to that extent there is sanctity that is inviolable. More recently there has been some turbulence about this commitment and the security of the minorities in India. Let me state this unambiguously. Apart from the sanctity that derives from the Constitution, today more than ever, the commitment to, and the practice of secularism, is a security imperative for a country like India. The societal ozone layer has been put to severe stress and we have to be ever vigilant that this remains intact. And this aspect is relevant for all multi-religious and diverse societies and states that are guided by the values of pluralism and democracy—such as the USA.

I first visited the USA when I was under 25—that is almost half a century ago. At the time the quip was that the people to people contact between the USA and India was great—but the government-to-government relationship was strained and both sides were suspicious of each other. Today we have come a long way from that impasse. The Indian diaspora in the USA has contributed in no small measure to the improvement in the bilateral relationship and the quip today is that the government to government or the so called Track One relationship has forged ahead of the Track Two—the non-governmental. Yet another lighter vein reference is that the relationship is so stable that the US Ambassador to India can offer a constructive critique and friendly advice in public and no one here invokes the 'foreign hand'!

Please do not be under the impression that what I am outlining is an idealistic and hopelessly optimistic scenario about the India-US relationship. No, I am not. I am reasonably experienced in matters of state conduct and subscribe to the view that all states are amoral and pursue what they perceive is in their self-interest. The challenge is when short-term benefits are prioritized over abiding long-term interests. Yes, on occasion Faustian bargains are made—but the system self-regulates and makes correction.

In the India-US case, I believe that the strategic convergences make for an ethical choice, I opted out of the seminary very early in life—but here I define ethics as enlightened self-interest. Today combating terrorism and supporting the concert of plural democracies, while managing economic liberalization and free markets with due concern for the human condition is the new referent. The strategic interests of India and the USA need to be identified and pursued in this context and a lot of hard work needs to be done by the professional and the academic. I urge the members of this distinguished audience to objectively interrogate the formulation I have outlined and contribute in your own way to the furtherance of India's overall national security Sinews. This would be apt tribute to the memory of the late General Bipin Joshi.

11

Kashmir: Past, Present and the Future

General K.V. Krishna Rao,
PVSM,
Chief of the Army Staff

Introduction

When I was asked to deliver the General B.C. Joshi Memorial Lecture, I felt it somewhat odd, as having been much younger to me, in the natural course of things, it is he who should have delivered a memorial lecture in my honour, and not the other way round: unfortunately, Providence snatched away this fine military leader who had considerable potential. I had known BC, as we used to fondly call him, ever since he was my cadet at the National Defence Academy, of which, I happened to be a Founder-Member. He was awarded the President's Gold Medal at the Academy, which shows that we were not wrong in assessing cadets as future leaders in the Armed Forces. Joshi had a distinguished career in the Army, having been Director of Military Operations, a Corps Commander in the troubled North-East, Army Commander in the South and West, and finally Chief of the Army Staff, at a time when the nation was faced with a serious crisis in Kashmir. We worked together, and although he passed away, success was ultimately achieved, in the way of crushing militancy and holding credible elections after a gap of seven years. Throughout his career, Joshi displayed professionalism of a high order, vision and patriotic fervour; and was worth emulation by other officers. I would like to compliment the prestigious Pune University and Headquarters Southern Command for organizing this lecture every year.

Coming to the subject of my lecture, at the outset. I would like to stress that Kashmir is not only an internal issue, but also a problem with international ramifications. It is the most intricate problem, which has defied a solution for the past 53 years, and is posing a serious challenge to the integrity of the nation. Like the-North East, it has great strategic significance. To be able to comprehend the problem, it is necessary to understand the important developments of the past, the present situation and visualize the likely future scenario.

Background

While the State of Jammu and Kashmir has been through several vicissitudes during its long history like the rest of India, I shall focus your attention on certain aspects that are still relevant and will remain so in the future too.

(a) The area was originally inhabited by Hindus, but Islam really spread in the region in the 14th century when Muslims came into power. The population of Muslims is estimated to be about 55 per cent, while Hindus constitute over 40 per cent and Buddhists and others the remainder. Thus, although the State had a Muslim majority, it was under Dogra rulers prior to independence.

(b) While the Muslim Conference formed in 1931 could not secure much relief from the autocratic rulers, after conversion to National Conference embracing all communities in 1939 under Sheikh Mohammad Abdullah, the struggle gained momentum in conjunction with the leaders of India's national struggle against the British. In 1946, when Jinnah tried to woo the Kashmiri leaders to join the proposed State of Pakistan, he was rebuffed. The National Conference found that there was greater convergence of ideals and interests with the Indian National Congress.

(c) After the partition of the subcontinent, despite a standstill agreement, Pakistan invaded the State on 20 October 1947. The Maharaja then acceded to India on 26 October, with the support of Sheikh Abdullah. While Indian troops dispatched to clear the State secured two thirds of the area, one third remained under Pakistani control at the time the ceasefire was announced 1 January 1949. A ceasefire line was delineated under the Karachi Agreement of 27 July 1949 which went from Manawar in the south to a point Khor NJ 9842 and thereafter it was to follow further north to the glaciers (Siachen).

(d) While the Operations were in progress, India approached the United Nations on 30 December 1947 to have the aggression vacated. According to UN Resolutions of 13 August 1948 and 5 January 1949, Pakistan was to withdraw all her forces from the State of Jammu and Kashmir, after which India was to reduce her forces, and after this was done, the future status of the State was to be determined by a plebiscite under the aegis of the United Nations. However, Pakistan never implemented the first part of the UN Resolution, but keeps propagating that India is not permitting self-determination in the State.

(e) In order to extend democracy to the State, elections were held to a Constituent Assembly, and a Constitution was drawn up for the State, based on which elections have been held to the Legislative Assembly regularly and people have elected governments of their choice. Section 3 of the Constitution declares "The State of Jammu and Kashmir is and shall be an integral part of the Union of India." Section 4 says "The territory of the State shall comprise all the territories which on the 15th day of August 1947, were under the Sovereignty or suzerainty of the ruler of the State."

(f) Article 370 of the Constitution of India defines the special relationship of the State with India, and envisages a considerable degree of autonomy. The relationship of the State with the rest of the country was further discussed between Sheikh Abdullah and Pandit Nehru and an agreement known as the 'Delhi Agreement' was arrived at in July 1952. However, Sheikh Abdullah was arrested on 8 August 1953 on the suspicion that he was working for the independence of Kashmir. Subsequently a number of provisions of the National Constitution were extended to the State, through the medium of Constitution Application Orders, with the concurrence of the State

Government in power at the time. The National Conference considers that these had eroded autonomy to a considerable extent.

(g) After a long incarceration, the Sheikh was released and the Indira-Sheikh Accord was arrived at. The Sheikh came back to power in February 1975. Under this accord, the National Conference could take up with the Centre any proposal for a review of the laws extended to the State after 1953, on any matter relatable to the Concurrent List. However, the State Government had not taken up any such matters with the Union Government. On the demise of Sheikh Abdullah on 8 September 1982, his son Dr. Farooq Abdullah came to power.

(h) The Farooq Government was dismissed on 2 July 1984 on the plea that he had lost support, and his brother-in-law Ghulam Mohammad Shah was appointed as Chief Minister. Subsequently he was also dismissed on 7 March 1986 on the plea of his inability to maintain law and order and President's rule was imposed.

(i) Subsequently, an agreement known as the Rajiv-Farooq Accord was reached on 6 November 1986. Farooq formed an Alliance Government with the Congress. In the elections held on 23 March 1987, Farooq got a considerable majority, but there were allegations that the elections had been rigged on a massive scale, that there was rampant corruption and so on and a violent agitation ensued.

Pakistan, not being reconciled to the status quo in Kashmir, launched two more aggressions in 1965 and 1971, preceded on both occasions by massive infiltration. However, its efforts were frustrated by the Indian Armed Forces. After each of these wars, there were peace agreements, namely, the Tashkent Agreement on 10 January 1966 and the Simla Agreement on 2 July 1972. However, Pakistan never adhered to these agreements after getting back her prisoners and territories. Taking advantage of the disturbed situation in the State, Pakistan evolved a new strategy of promoting a proxy war. A large number of disgruntled youth were lured to Pakistan, trained, armed, equipped, funded, indoctrinated and infiltrated into Jammu and Kashmir to rise in rebellion. When the Government at the Centre changed in December 1989, and the

Alliance Government in the State resigned, President's Rule was declared on 19 January 1990. As the situation started deteriorating, particularly due to the release of some hard-core militants, in exchange for the Union Home Minister's daughter who had been kidnapped, Pakistan took full advantage to boost up militancy.

The Proxy War

As a result of militancy, all the organs of the State were subverted. The administration was paralysed, the police became ineffective and involved with militants, politicians deserted to safer havens and a number of leaders were assassinated. Considerable devastation took place such as the burning of schools, bridges and dispensaries, education and tourism was disrupted while the economy suffered grievous damage. The minority community migrated, the media carried out the dictates of the militants and the public were terrorized, confused and uncertain of their future. In other words, the militants were able to gain the upper hand and a parallel government was being run by them.

In March 1993, it was decided that the deteriorating situation should be arrested, militancy crushed, and the authority of the Government re-established. Elections were to be held thereafter and democracy restored. A multipronged approach was adopted for the purpose, which comprised of four major thrusts. These were; a vigorous anti-militancy drive, making the administration more responsive, revival of political activity and winning back the people.

As a result of these measures, about 8,000 militants were killed, 33,000 were captured, a huge number of weapons were recovered, and militancy was crushed by June 1995. A conducive atmosphere was created for conducting elections.

Revival of Democracy

Thereafter, parliamentary elections were held in May 1996 and Assembly elections in September. The National Conference secured a two-thirds majority and a government under Dr. Farooq Abdullah was sworn in on 9 October 1996. It may be mentioned that there was about 60 per cent turnout in the elections, which have been accepted as credible by the international community.

Several challenges lay ahead for the State Government, and the Chief Minister was advised to deal with them promptly and effectively. These included prevention of a second proxy war succeeding, providing a responsive administration, rebuilding the State Police, returning and resettling the migrants, rehabilitating militancy victims, reconstructing of damaged assets, reviving of tourism and sick industries, overhauling the education system, extending democracy to the grass-roots level, tackling the unemployment problem, eliminating corruption and nepotism, and so on. In other words, the Government had to provide a competent, clean and responsive administration. The Godbole Committee constituted later submitted a very useful report, which could be implemented to advantage.

The Centre also had important responsibilities in restoring full normalcy and carrying the people of the State with it. Broadly, these included full support in the way of forces required for maintaining peace, finances for reconstruction, rehabilitation and revival, assistance in solving unemployment problem, cleaning up the administration and police, discouraging all talk of abrogation of Article 370, resolving the autonomy issue without jeopardizing national interests, and bringing diplomatic pressure on Pakistan to restrain it from interfering in Jammu and Kashmir, and seeking the co-operation of all parties to treat Jammu and Kashmir as a national problem, and so on.

Pakistani Machinations

Restoration of democracy in the State meant a defeat for Pakistan in the proxy war, as it was proved that the Kashmiris were very much with India and that Pakistan was rebuffed once again. After this, Pakistan was in jitters for some time and was in a quandary as to what to do, as evident from not only intercepts but also their newspapers. It is difficult to say how far the State and the Centre succeeded in their efforts to bring back full normalcy and maintain the requisite grip. As per media reports, the people appear to be alienated once again, their expectations not having been probably met. Pakistan seems to have taken advantage of the situation and staged a number of incidents, including attacks on military camps and using an increasing number of foreign mercenaries and suicide squads. However, finding that even the recrudescence of such depredations had not brought about a substantial change in the situation, Pakistan resorted to the Kargil intrusion, in the hope that it could compel India to negotiate for Kashmir.

In the Kargil area, Pakistani forces occupied certain unmanned heights in the gaps between Indian pickets, over an area of about 150 kilometres, perhaps to isolate Ladakh. Initially, it took some time for the local forces to realize the gravity of the situation. According to Pakistan, they had planned the operation in October 1998 and occupied the heights in February 1999. However, the intrusion, as such, was discovered only in May 1999. Requisite forces had to be inducted and operations launched over a period to clear the aggression, but at considerable cost. Further, additional forces, including Corps Headquarters and an additional division, had to be permanently committed in the area. The Kargil Review Committee brought out certain lacunae and lessons such as failure of Intelligence, inadequate vigilance, deficiencies in weapons and equipment, ineffective management of national security, and so on. The Army had appointed its own committee as well to go into the mishap. It is hoped that proper lessons have been drawn honestly and that there will be no recurrence of such incidents.

The Kargil incident was followed by a civilian coup and a military counter-coup in Pakistan in October 1999. The Pakistani Supreme Court has set a time limit for the return of democracy and the Chief Executive Officer, General Pervez Musharraf, has been saying that he will abide by the judgment. Irrespective of whether he does so or not, it has to be realized that in Pakistan, the military has over-riding influence, whether there is democracy or not. This aspect, as also the fact that Indian governments in the past did deal with military dictators, needs to be remembered when considering the question of talks.

The other development that took place was the hijacking incident in December 1999. There was an opportunity to effectively deal with the hijackers in Amritsar on 24 December 1999, but this was not exploited. The exchange of some top hard-core militants with the passengers at Kandahar had created a very adverse impact, both internally and externally. Such incidents will continue to happen and an effective policy needs to be evolved.

In July 2000, there was an offer of ceasefire and talks with the Indian Government by the Hizbul Mujahideen, the major militant outfit in

Kashmir. However, because of its insistence on the talks being tripartite with the participation of Pakistan, and to be outside the Indian Constitution, India could not agree. It would appear that Pakistan, having failed to get India to talk directly with it, had engineered the proposal by the Hizbul. The Jamat-a-Islami Pakistan, which controls the Hizbul Mujahideen, is itself suspicious of the Pakistani Government's intentions.

The Future

About 111,370 square kilometres of territory is under Pakistani occupation in Jammu and Kashmir and about 13,000 square kilometres under Chinese occupation in Ladakh. Further, Pakistan has made offer of about 4,500 square kilometres of territory to China in the Karakoram area, through which a major highway has been developed by China connecting Xinxiang with Gilgit. There are Parliament Resolutions in the case of both Pakistan and China, which express the Indian resolve to retrieve these territories, no matter how long it may take. Further, in both cases, it was Pakistan and China who committed the aggression and India was the victim. Both Pakistan and China display a resolve to hold on to these territories; and not only that, they have advanced further claims on Indian territory. These aspects have to be kept in view, while considering any solution for the Kashmir problem. It should not result in the old Arab and camel story.

Pakistan considers that Kashmir is the unfinished business of Partition and is the core dispute between the two countries. Not only that, it has rejected any settlement along the Line of Control. What it wants at the least is the whole of the Kashmir Valley and all the Muslim majority areas that include the districts of Poonch, Rajouri, Doda and Kargil. That would leave India in a precarious position from a strategic point of view, apart from the people not wanting to throw their lot with Pakistan.

As far as China is concerned, its Western Highway linking Tibet with Xinxiang passes through the Aksai Chin area. Apart from Aksai Chin, she it has put forward claims on Arunachal Pradesh and certain small areas along the northern border, does not recognize Sikkim as part of India and resents India's Defence Treaty with Bhutan. China is not even keen on delineating the Line of Actual Control, leave alone resolution of the border problem. It opposes India's seat in the Security Council, although India supported China's entry into the United Nations. Further, it wants India to roll back its nuclear programme. The nexus between China and Pakistan is well known.

Under the circumstances, what are the options available to Pakistan, to achieve its aim?

(a) Get the support of the United Nations for a plebiscite, on the plea of self-determination being denied to the Kashmiris as envisaged in the UN resolutions. Presently, with international opinion veering more towards India, this may not be possible.

(b) Get third-party intervention, mainly of the USA, on the plea that bilateral talks would not solve the problem due to India's 'intransigence'. This may not be possible without India's concurrence, which may not be given. In any case, the Clinton visit could not have generated much hope in this regard in Pakistan.

(c) Strive for talks with India and insist on at least Muslim majority areas being transferred to Pakistan. India is unlikely to accept such a proposition.

(d) If this is not possible, get India to regularize the line of control as the permanent border. With international pressure on India to settle the problem somehow and some internal pressure, India may consider such a proposal. However, Pakistan may find it difficult to justify such a compromise, particularly to its fundamentalist elements and the Army.

(e) Continue the proxy war to force India to come to the negotiating table. Depending on India's ability to handle the proxy war, the success could vary.

(f) Launch a full-fledged attack on Kashmir in the hope that the nuclear capability will prevent India from crossing the international borders. A war confined to the mountains alone will be very protracted and expensive; and Pakistan will not be able to achieve its aim. Further, there is no guarantee that India will not cross the borders in retaliation and thus extend the war, keeping in view its own superior nuclear capability. Further, Pakistan will not have the support of the international community for such an adventure.

There is considerable pressure on India to agree to talk with Pakistan. As I mentioned earlier, it is immaterial whether India talks to the military government or waits for a civilian government to emerge, as the military has a predominant influence on national affairs in that country. However, should talks take place, India should be clear as to how far it is prepared to go, that is, the 'bottom line', in trying to find an enduring solution to the problem. For this purpose, it would be better if a national consensus is developed on the issue. The sanctity of the Parliament resolutions also needs to be kept in view.

As any permanent solution to the Kashmir problem is likely to take a long time, India must ensure that internally, stability is achieved and a full grip is maintained on the situation in Jammu and Kashmir. In fact, this will help in dealing with the external problem better. For this purpose, while taking firm measures against militancy and maintaining control, talks should be held with all parties, including militant groups that are prepared to talk, as well as the Hurriyat, on the question of autonomy. It needs to be remembered that a certain amount of autonomy was provided for right from the beginning, by way of Article 370, the Delhi Agreement, the Indira-Sheikh Accord, and the promises made by successive governments before the 1996 elections in Jammu and Kashmr. Talks on autonomy do not mean that anything is conceded, which goes against national vital interests. In fact, Farooq himself has indicated that his party would be flexible in the discussions. Equally, early decisions should be taken by the State Government on internal autonomy for the three regions, as demands for trifurcation and constitution of separate States is gaining momentum, and is not in the interest of the State or the country. Concurrently, every effort should be made to make the administration more efficient and responsive, and find employment for the large number of unemployed youth, even outside the State. Overall, Jammu and Kashmir needs to be managed much more efficiently, in order to carry the people with the rest of the country. Experience has shown that the people will co-operate when they are convinced that their life, identity and future are safe in Indian hands.

A war is a costly affair, and should be avoided if possible but the country should be fully prepared at all times, in case it is thrust upon it, to be able to give a fitting reply to the enemy. However, to be able to do so, we need a suitable national security organization, which has not been allowed to emerge by vested interests. Certain recommendations have been made in this regard and an effective organization must take shape, in order to protect and promote our national vital interests. Otherwise, the country will find itself seriously endangered, and those responsible will have to answer to the nation.

12

Indigenous Science & Technology in the Shaping of Air Power for National Security

Air Chief Marshal A.Y. Tipnis,
AVSM, VM, ADC CAS,
Chief of the Air Staff

Pune University has done me, and through me, the Indian Air Force, a singular honour by inviting me to deliver the Late Gen. B.C. Joshi Memorial Oration. A General of extraordinarily high repute and a passionate scholar of military history, strategy and war studies, he applied himself vigorously to innovative thinking on national security and defence strategy. But for his untimely demise, he would have achieved many more credits in this field in his capacity as the Chief of Army Staff. I was fortunate to attend one of his addresses soon after he took over as the Chief. His vision on the impact of science and technology on future human conflicts and the shaping of national security were unique and perhaps even prophetic. Pune University has done well to perpetuate his legacy by establishing this lecture series in his memory. I hope I am able to adequately honour his memory and justify the trust placed in my capability by the University.

As I stand here, I can't help but wonder what on earth I am doing here, having the temerity to address a gathering of eminent personalities, and experts. How can I possibly make myself bold to preach to the high priests of industry, science, technology defence, national security and I am sure in a host of other fields of expertise on a subject that may touch all these areas? But assuming that the Vice Chancellor would not really have relented and withdrawn his invitation, even if I had my sense of inadequacy known to him, here I am. Be assured, I won't preach; I will only share some of my thoughts, some of which may be bordering on anxieties. But I do seek your indulgence, if I leave behind more questions than answers.

The commonly accepted definition of national security is that of safeguarding the sovereignty and territorial integrity of the nation-state. Some enlightened and benevolent scholars have also attempted to give a more people-centred view by calling national security the state's and citizen's concern with safeguarding the way of life of the people. The first definition creates the impression that national security entails only the creation of adequately strong defence forces to thwart an external aggression. I am sure that this impression is only strengthened when a man in uniform is about to delve on this subject. At the very outset, I want this august audience to allow me go beyond this tight framework and make for a wider understanding on national security. I also want to ponder on the implications and the demands of the second definition of national security—but here again I would like to expand the framework of the definition. National security calls on the state and the citizens to not only safeguard the existing way of life, but also uplift it to a higher quality and reducing personal risk in everyday life.

When one talks of science, again the tendency is to think of only the technical process of experimentation with material things and physics. Technology conjures up visions of mechanisation and automation. Technical sciences, technology, together with human and sociological sciences must be applied in equal measure for the development of human resources, quality of life, the strengthening of national life, promotion of harmony, eradication of poverty and healing of fissiparous forces. We must accept that many of the issues that have been politicised could have been avoided can perhaps be rectified in the future by more enlightened development in the field of human sciences.

Similarly, when one talks of indigenous technical modernisation, one is inclined to think of only top-of-the-line and frontier technologies—medium, low and even what I call nitty-gritty technologies—if I may indulge in a brief illustration of what I mean. Look at the state of our bullock-carts, cycle rickshaws, *'thelewala'* kiosks, public transport and literally a million other things. Hopefully we will wake up to the nightmares of the inadequacy of the road architecture for Indian traffic conditions and the quality of life that our town planning or lack of it offers.

No, don't fear, I will stay on track with the main theme of my talk. These short references to things non-military were to indicate that we in uniform are not concerned merely with arms and ammunition. Amongst a host of claims that can justifiably be made for giving a sobriquet to the 20th century, I think science and technology on the one hand and air power on the other, can indeed be the front-running contenders for this honour. As this century fades away it will continue to be long remembered as the century of Science and Technology and for its contribution to the development of our power. And I do believe that the 21st century will continue to be seized with the development of science and technology in every sphere of human endeavour as never before and will stake its claim as the Century of Aerospace Power.

National development and national defence have to be planned and exercised in conjunction. Neither of the two can be true, strong and progressive without the equal development of the other. Adequate national development alone can provide the required needs for defence and unless our defence is secure, national development can never be optimised and our national destiny shaped, as we truly desire.

Our early legacy in defence planning was not quite so inspiring. The British Defence Planning process for India did not involve much public debate on the allocation for defence and the distribution of this allocation. The Indian forces were structured to complement and supplement the British forces in India for maintenance of internal and external security, the total cost of which apparently remained apart from the amount available for development. Possibly this legacy was responsible for the policy on defence through the early years after independence and the expenditure on defence remained "non-plan".

Our importance to defence or possibly the lack of it is starkly revealing from our expenditure on it through the years. At the start of the first decade after independence, we spent 1.7 per cent of the GDP on defence. At the start of the next decade, it had gone up marginally to 2.0 per cent, but rose sharply through 3 per cent in 1962-63 to 4.5 per cent in 1963-64, the peak of our defence expenditure, but then settled down to around 3.5 per cent. In the last few years, it has stagnated at less than 2.8 per cent. I think there is a strong case for increasing it to more than 3.0 per cent, perhaps it could be closer to 3.5 per cent. There is a case for wider discussion and debate on the subject. Besides the debate on the overall defence budgeting, I think it is in order to delve on the distribution of the available finance. After all it is binding on us that we acquire the highest deterrence value and the most assured winning capability for every rupee that we spend.

Our objective in maximising our self-reliance on defence can be achieved only if the national plan achieves the scientific, technological and industrial base to genuinely support, both in quality and quantity, the development needs of the country as a whole, inclusive of the developmental needs of the country including its defence effort and its defence-oriented industrial effort.

The dawn of the century saw the birth of aviation; at its sunset we are experiencing the establishment of air power as the ultimate arbiter of human conflict. Air power is able to do today what its protagonists foresaw almost as soon as the first hand-held bomb left an airborne vehicle. The Gulf War saw the air campaign last for 38 days before the Allied ground forces were committed. The havoc caused from the air made way for the ground forces to over-run the disarrayed and demoralized Iraqi Army in less than a hundred hours. Kosovo saw the NATO forces keep their hands completely on the ground and achieved their military objectives with air power alone. But I do hasten to acknowledge that despite the virtual total absence of air opposition, the strength of 1,000 ac still required 11 weeks of intensive campaigning. We have to also note that the weather placed severe limitations on the application of combat power through the medium of the air.

While the argument that the Iraq and Kosovo wars, unless analysed more objectively, could mislead to wrong conclusions in our context is well taken, the emergence of air power as the most effective deterrence and the one with the most potent war winning capability has to be acknowledged.

Even our own experience substantiates this. In 1947-48, the air support to the Army, both in its timely induction into Kashmir and in close air support, was helpful to it in pushing out the Pakistanis from the Valley. The Pakistani armour thrusts, both in 1965 and 1971, were blunted effectively from the air. The total air superiority over the erstwhile East Pakistan allowed our ground advance virtually unopposed. The suddenness of the surrender of the East Pakistan Forces could well be attributed to the effectiveness of the precisely timed air attack on the Governor's house in Dhaka.

Much closer in time are the recent Kargil operations. Evicting the Pakistanis from their elevated dominating positions was a herculean task. Our army casualties would have been much higher had not air action demolished several rear supply points (Muntho-Dhalo and Point 4388 to name the two most in the news); had air action not shaken the forward positions (Tiger Hill and Tololing are no doubt familiar names to all those present here), and had air power not broken the morale of the enemy by attacking their positions by day and by night and even when they may have felt secure under the cover of clouds. Let me tell you that at one time, it was even doubted whether the eviction was at all possible and there were contingencies being considered for undertaking offensives elsewhere, until air power dealt the telling blows. Let no Indian believes that Musharraf withdrew from his position because of political pressure on him; he sought withdrawal because aerial action made his positions untenable. With the PAF not being able to take the pressure off from the air, the Pak army could not possibly have faced it alone. There were some meek attempts by the PAF to interfere, but seeing our strong AD presence, better sense prevailed in them and kept them away from the conflict.

The deadliness of air power has gained and will continue to gain greater lethality through the application of newer and more refined older technologies. The application of the scientific means in a host of independent and inter-related fields will allow faster, far superior and more cost-effective training resulting in synergising all elements into a force-multiplying effect that is far greater than the sum total of all. It is my purpose this evening to consider some of the various possibilities in the shaping of air power today and forecasting its shape for tomorrow.

I have articulated earlier that air power has emerged as the ultimate arbiter of human conflicts. I grant some may wish to take up cudgels on the issue; but I do believe that they will readily accept that it is the most lethal power and certainly, in the case of advanced nations, the preferred means of waging war. But as has been our experience, wars will not always be fought in expected places or for that matter in the traditional manner. I think we have to accept that we have to be prepared for waging wars and operations in varying degrees of spectrum conflict. I think air power has the flexibility to adapt to these contingencies of high, medium and low levels of this spectrum with essentially the same type and structure of the force. I would categorise the Kargil Operation in the low end of the conflict spectrum. There have been questions on whether the IAF missed the availability of slower speed combat aircraft. I am happy to respond that all the fleets put into action in Kargil performed eminently well. Their high performance kept them out of harm's way of the shoulder-fired missiles. Our innovative adaptation of the GPS gave us the capability to attack cloud-covered targets with MiG-27s and MiG-21s by day and by night. Our technical capability allowed us to modify aircraft rapidly with GPS and counter measure devices.

I have made a mention of these technical achievements, albeit not spectacular, under operational conditions, to underscore the obvious importance of self-reliance and indigenous capability. In this age of progressive technological development, aircraft, weapons and self-defence systems are continuously in need of upgradation. Without a quarrel, everyone would like to go indigenously all the way. But two factors need careful consideration: the level of sophistication that we are able to achieve, and the level of assurance that can be given in maintaining cost and time estimates. An upgradation due to its delay in induction must not only be not outdated, but also have a sufficient in-service useful life. While for years we have been undertaking many projects in collaboration, it is my belief that despite our best efforts the progress of projects is not maintained as planned and/or the know-how on base technologies does not get transferred to the extent we seek; unless the collaborator has a stake in it and is equally dependent on us for part development this is always likely to happen. Perhaps we can have joint projects, which are required by both partners with equal urgency. By sharing the development of responsibilities more or less equally, both partners can combat their vulnerability to information blocking by following the same tactic, if required. This is not to say that we should be chary of joint ventures, but we have to be aware of the pitfalls and take practical steps to overcome them.

One of the biggest challenges before the IAF is to expand the indigenous maintenance capability and reduce our spare dependability on manufacturing of original equipment. In respect of indigenous servicing for spares, we are making a very concerted effort, both to create and increase in-house depot level manufacture and make use of the private sector to meet as much of our demand as possible. The Confederation of Indian Industries has been particularly supportive in this drive of ours. The response has been generally limited to low-technology items. I do believe that this is a national challenge and Indian industries must rise to it. For our part, we are simplifying procedures to help accelerate the process of initiation, but I say to the captains of industry, do not be put off by the stringency of specifications. I think industry could also look at the repair of our mechanical, electrical and electronic rotables and components. We have had some successes in reverse engineering as well as ingenuity in designing in-lieu parts for some of the components. But a lot more needs to be done. The IAF will ever welcome reconsideration from the industry to strengthen and widen our national capability.

There are many other areas which I think can be taken up by the private sector in collaboration with the public sector or independently, possibly in competition. Stimulation and virtual reality have vast scope for supporting and modernising our pilot and technical training. Today, development in the field of virtual reality can facilitate combat crew to most realistically rehearse an entire mission. Such rehearsals will increase mission accomplishment probability and assurance manifold and help drastically reduce attrition. Our national strength in software development surely makes this possible well within our independent capability. Improved and sophisticated war-gaming software can and must improve the quality and speed of decision-making.

In the new wars, time will be the biggest force multiplier with the high weapon carrying capability of today's aircraft and extreme precision of weapons and target neutralisation will be achieved by only a fraction of the force level required earlier. This should increase manifold the capability to take on more targets. The limiting factors here could well be the ability or rather the inability to produce target information and mission tasking orders fast enough, computer-based target analysis and formulation of tasking orders can do the necessary speeding up. Again, we must be able to exploit fully our well-established software development capabilities.

As an aviator, I have referred to only the aviation sector for gainful application of our indigenous science and technology. Even if, just in passing, may I venture to say that there is an equal need, if not more, to apply gainfully our advancement in science and technology to non-military fields to modernise our infrastructure which will help our national security, our housing, buildings, city roads, town planning including mass communication means, inter-city communications, to put it bluntly, are all primitive and waste a colossal amount of useful man-hours in doing the chores of daily life. It is maddening the amount of time and effort that military commanders have to spend in attempting to give a reasonable quality of life, not the least of which is ordinary cleanliness. Keeping the environment decent must be made easier. Let me emphasise that these are not peripheral things; the morale of our men in uniform is involved.

During my talk I have attempted to make a case for co-ordinated effort for national development and defence preparedness. There is an inter-dependence between the two and that in fact, only adequate defence preparedness will allow for smooth national development. This was led on with a plea for adequate budget allocation for defence. A shortfall in adequacy of allocation will have long-term repercussions, which will not be easily rectifiable. Division of the defence budget between the three elements needs to be reviewed to ensure that we do in fact get the defence state that we desire within the available funding. It is my belief, based on historical events, that air power will be the dominant combat power of the future, both as a deterrent and as a war-winning force. I have tried to touch upon some of the aspects that indigenous science, technology and industry need to consider in our endeavour to meet defence needs.

In conclusion, I would say that India's place in the 21st century will depend upon the corrective action that we take on our recognisable weaknesses and proceed with great vigour on our strengths. I think with our native intelligence and propensity for hard work, we have every right to hope for a more secure future, perhaps with better understanding of strengths and weaknesses of different agencies, along with dynamic and effective co-ordination leading to more positive results, which we are looking for.

13

India: Renaissance 2000?

General Shankar Roy Chowdhury,
PVSM, ADC,
Chief of the Army Staff

I am very pleased to be here this evening on the occasion of the annual General B.C. Joshi Memorial Lecture. Such an event is an eminently appropriate method of remembering General Bipin Chandra Joshi, my predecessor in the office of Chief of the Army Staff, a most distinguished soldier, a military intellectual, and, above all, an ardent patriot.

It is a privilege to address this distinguished audience here at the University of Pune, an august institution of learning, which is commemorating fifty golden and distinguished years of its existence, though I am well aware that the histories of many of its constituent colleges go back a good deal longer than that. Amongst my more prominent recollections of General Joshi is his firm and unshakable belief, which he frequently expressed, that he saw eight special signs which indicated that the next century (now just little more than a year away), would be India's century. I used to be quite intrigued by this statement and sometimes asked him what these signs were, and how would they manifest themselves? Unfortunately, as he was untimely snatched away by the hand of fate, the opportunity to progress the discussion further never arose.

We have just commemorated fifty years of our existence as an independent nation state. In the new millennium, more than ever before in history, our national well-being and security will increasingly rest on the three interlinked cantilevers of Economic Prosperity, Social Stability, and National Security, which together constitute National Power. Our fortunes and experiences in all the three areas have been mixed. We have made substantial progress on some issues, but have not been able to achieve matching success in others. Overall, however, there can be no doubt that we have made considerable progress.

Our goal of economic prosperity for a nation cannot be merely about economics alone, because true prosperity requires a strong social content as well. Countries cannot be run like department stores, and it is not possible to provide satisfactory governance to anything as complex as a modern society solely by application of sheer economic technology. Rather, economic prosperity has to be a more overarching view about the general well-being and prosperity of the nation and the people, which mere economic growth by itself often fails to deliver. The concept of national prosperity has to embrace both the science of economics and the humanity of the social sciences, interlinking and incorporating various aspects of the social environment with nationwide growth and development of industry, agriculture, science and technology.

After decades of centralized planning in a controlled economy, we have begun to adopt the principles of the free market as the path to a better life for our people. But its promised trickle-down benefits appear to have difficulty in percolating down to the nation's rural grassroots where the majority of our people live in grinding poverty and deprivation. Many will ascribe this to faulty or half-hearted implementation of a free market economy, but experience in other developing countries seems to suggest that the exclusively fiscal-oriented approach of the free market does not, indeed cannot, really afford to have any kind of a social face. Unrestrained and thoughtless application of cowboy capitalism from the Wild West to developing societies across the world, has everywhere resulted in massive job losses, unemployment, land alienation, and tensions of economic disparities leading to rising crime, degeneration of public support systems, and environmental degradation—the so called "growing pains" of a market economy, with deferred promises of a brighter future. But it ignores the worsening realities of the present, in a viciously competitive, no-holds-barred, financial bottom-line approach, which has triggered off food riots, unemployment marches, and other major social upheavals. These have affected the internal stability of an increasing number of countries across the world from South America to Eastern Europe. The erstwhile Asian Tigers like Indonesia, Malaysia, and Thailand are in the throes of the worst social crises in their history. Russia and some of the Central Asian Republics are rapidly becoming ungovernable. Even First World bastions like Germany are affected by record unemployment, while in the USA, small traditional family farms are being gradually wiped out under burdens of debt. It appears that with the current economic dispensation, the problems of small farmers in Andhra Pradesh, Maharashtra, and Punjab, are common to their counterparts in Wyoming, North Dakota, and Montana as well. Popular disillusionment with the siren song of get-rich-quick economic theories has generated a bitter harvest in many countries that had rushed to adopt them in frenzied haste. Economic policies which till recently were considered to be irreparably obsolete, are now under re-examination once again. There must be a lesson in all this for our own country, and there a rising chorus of voices urging a pause to review and rethink our options. We must pay heed to them.

India's experiences in the Great International Bazaar have not been entirely pleasant or beneficial either. It has become very evident that the so-called First World is not promoting free market mantras out of pure concern for a better world future. Free trade and free markets appear to be acceptable to the developed nations only as long as the underdeveloped countries of the so-called Third World are kept in their place as sources of raw materials, cheap labour, and markets for glossy consumer products, to maintain the economies and lifestyle of the First World. But where there is even the smallest possibility of this flow being reversed by competition from cheaper finished goods manufactured at lower rates by less expensive Third World economies, non-tariff barriers are all being increasingly deployed by the developed countries. Subjective quasi-moral interpretations of issues like environmental degradation, child labour, human rights, and selective applications of health and quality standards, are being cynically exploited by the so-called First World to protect their own domestic industries and jobs from what is seen as unfairly low-priced competition from less developed economies. Preservation of their own farmers and working classes is paramount in all countries, especially where elected governments are dependent on their votes. Thus, in a strange distortion of democracy, peasants and workers in many developed countries have become well entrenched pressure groups totally opposed to free market flows of goods and services wherever their own interests are affected. In the so-called European Union, French farmers block roads and harbours to stop imports of cheaper farm products from neighbouring countries, fishing wars flare up in the North Atlantic between English, French and Spanish fishermen, the USA refuses entry to Indian software engineers, while Japan refuses entry to the American car industry and even mobilizes patriotic sentiments at home to market Japanese products. Closer to home, Japanese, Korean and Taiwanese fishing vessels in the Bay of Bengal and the Arabian Sea are driving Indian fishermen out of the market. Indian exports, already marginal by international volumes, are being further affected by the increasing virulence of what is actually unstated economic warfare.

Economic self-reliance was one of the basic strategies of our freedom struggle, and is now crucial to the renaissance of the nation. It has become absolutely essential to put the country on a firm footing in the bitterly competitive no-holds-barred world of a free market economy heavily slanted in favour of the developed countries. India is a large country, with a very large population base, and thus the natural advantage of a potentially gigantic internal market. This is an inherent economic strength, which if exploited judiciously, can in theory, make us into a self-contained economic fortress, unaffected by the vagaries of world economy. We have not exploited this with enough determination to extract the maximum benefits from our many assets. Mahatma Gandhi's spinning wheel is regarded with a degree of amused condescension by many corporate yuppies of the current generation. Their limited vision confuses the symbol with the substance. The charkha does not represent merely what it actually is, but symbolizes the goal of national self-reliance in industry, science and technology, be it production engineering, machine tools, bio-sciences, or nuclear technology.

Till relatively recently, the country's internal markets were closely regulated to keep direct international competition out, with the perfectly laudable aim of allowing indigenous Indian industry to build up and gather strength, and ultimately be in a competitive position in the international market. This was the route to economic super-stardom adopted with conspicuous success by Japan, today's free market giant where, incidentally, the Government played a dominating role in determining the growth pattern of the private sector. But the Indian corporate culture turned out to be different. Our industry readily accepted Government protection but also liked the taste of easy profits from monopoly markets, and, generally made no efforts to develop themselves into world-class competitiveness. With a very few honourable exceptions, our established industrialists in the post-Independence period displayed a cynical lack of concern for quality control, or promotion of indigenous research and development, or technology updates and gave short shrift to consumer satisfaction, with no thought beyond their own immediate short-term gains. Now that India seeks to join a globalised world economy and attract foreign investments, the Indian private sector is facing the heat of international competition. Some are fighting back to witness the international launch, fifty years late of course, of a new Indian designed small car. Others are agitating for level playing fields. There is no assurance that even if their requirements are met, they will not attempt to move the goalposts again. Many feel that Indian industry should simply be thrown in the deep end of free market competition to sink or swim as best as it can. The chances are that most will perish. The cynical and long suffering Indian consumer may therefore be forgiven for wishing them good riddance, if they are to be replaced by cheaper, higher quality foreign products, now available in plenty. But notwithstanding the wayward track record of Indian industry, strong internationally recognized indigenous brand names, whether in potato chips or in computer chips, are an essential component of the national mystique, and our national interests demand a strong indigenous industrial capability—Mitsubishi of Japan, Daimler-Benz of Germany, and General Motors of the USA are all integral parts of the national identities of their respective countries. India requires building up a similar identity for itself. Therefore, it is necessary to preserve Indian brand names in the national interest. The destruction of Indian industry by exposure to unequal competition in the world free market even after fifty years of misspent freedom would be a counterproductive knee-jerk reaction and against our national interests, figuratively amounting to cutting off the nose to spite the face. If our industry still requires level playing fields even after five decades of a protected market economy, the Government on its part must enforce a demanding regime of *quid pro quo* accountability and performance from industry, slapping safeguards and punitive sanctions, if necessary, to ensure this.

The nation had also sought to rapidly develop a large infrastructure in heavy industry through massive investments in the public sector at a time when the private sector in the country had limited capacity to do so. The results were initially spectacular, giving the country an array of core industrial assets with very substantial production capacities, which no other developing country possessed, and were also the envy of many of the so-called developed countries of the time. The public sector undertakings were designed to be very large state-owned production agencies, required at a time when the Government wanted to rapidly carry out major development and industrialization of the country. Logically, therefore, this sector should also have been the major, if not the sole beneficiary, of the large Government contracts and projects. But after establishing these major industrial units with substantial capital outlays of public money, the same Government, which should have been their chief patron and supporter, failed to follow up their early developmental phase with adequate organizational support and positive growth environment in terms of experienced management, responsible and responsive labour, and a professional industrial climate. Soon enough, all the ills of the governmental culture were visited on these industrial enterprises. The public sector was saddled with undisciplined, pampered trade unions controlled by irresponsible professional politicians, slow, unimaginative decision-making through bureaucratic remote control by the Government, and venal ministers who exploited the immense resources of these industries for personal and party benefits. More than the private sector, it was perhaps the public sector that required a level playing field with a greater degree of urgency. Under proper management, public sector industries in other countries have performed as well as and sometimes better than their counterparts in the private sector. But in India, they had failed, because they had really not been given a reasonable chance to prove themselves. Mass distress sales of valuable industrial assets in the government sector, as a sacrifice to the new gods of privatization is not in the national interest either. Rather, even at this late stage, the public sector must be refurbished with the right type of management, the trade unions disciplined, and the enterprises brought into the industrial mainstream.

Indigenous research and development followed a similar path. In the initial post-independence years, the Government had the vision and foresight to create a Council for Scientific and Industrial Research (CSIR), an Atomic Energy Commission (AEC), a Defence Research and Development Organization (DRDO), as well as more specialized agencies like the Indian Space Research Institute (ISRO) and others. Under them, a chain of high-grade research laboratories and technical institutions was created in almost all conceivable theoretical and applied disciplines for the promotion and application of science and technology by Indians for India. The Indian Institutes of Technology and the Indian Institutes of Management were established adhering to world-class standards. Our universities at the time of Independence were established educational institutions of good academic reputation with excellent faculty and contemporary research facilities. As a matter of fact, India entered her Independence with a wealth of scientific assets and potential not available even to many established nations of that time. But, as in other areas of national endeavour, we failed to follow up and capitalize on what a more determined nation would have taken as a flying head start. To begin with, our public and private sector industry did not have the resources to establish independent research facilities, nor indeed did they show any interest in doing so. But, rather than energise and utilize the indigenous facilities and resources already established in the country to develop product applications that could perhaps outsell world competitors, our industry preferred to acquire products of obsolete screwdriver technology from the West. As in the public sector industry, the organizations established for management of science soon imbibed the bureaucratic culture characteristic of all Government enterprises. Here again, we did not appear to be capable of developing a positive attitude towards enhancement of indigenous technology developed in a spirit of national endeavour.

Myopic political rivalry further muddied the waters by repeated re-examination and renegotiations of foreign collaborative projects already finalized by predecessor governments. These are acts of criminal folly whose erosive effect on our international credibility seems to be beyond the limited comprehension of small-time mofussil politicians coming to office through vote bank politics. Meanwhile, the politico-corporate nexus takes advantage of the trends for deregulation and continues to loot and misappropriate the financial resources entrusted to our commercial institutions for safe investment, resulting in an endless series of scams, which does not do much good to our image or reputation either.

So fifty years down the road, our national reach for economic prosperity through world class industrial and technology development have foundered in both the private and public sectors, through disinterest and strategic myopia, neglect and inefficient bureaucratized management, unashamed political interference, and militant, under productive labour. The lesson for us here is not about success or failure of one or the other economic system. All systems are only as good as the people who operate them, and in this, one system is as good as another is. Rather, it is about a historic setback to nation-building, caused by failure of collective human endeavour on a national scale, a refusal to see the overall good of the nation and society, flaws in the national character, if you like, which have jeopardized the long-term interests of the nation. We cannot afford these failures any longer, and must take the necessary hard decisions—legislative, fiscal, and legal measures—to stop or minimize such systems failures on a national scale. But all in all, there is a strong case for re-examination of the headlong rush for global integration at all costs.

Social stability is the fabric of national well-being. It flows from the confluence of good governance with well-developed perceptions of societal and national values, linked with economic prosperity. Our complex societal structure with six major religions, innumerable caste systems, fourteen major languages, and upward of five hundred dialects spoken in greater or lesser degree in various parts of the country, have generated competing pressures that have multiplied unchecked in a climate of permissiveness and licence. One of the features of the last fifty years has been the coming into being of India as a Republic, for the first time in our claimed history and mythology of around three to five thousand years. This is a very basic and rather obvious fact, which all of us unthinkingly take for granted, because, except for the minimal recent period, our history since the *Ramayana* or the *Mahabharata* era has all along been of centralized dynastic rule by kings and viceroys, and also by gods and demons as well. Such prolonged societal conditioning to particular socio-political culture of governance must have definitely exercised some effect on our collective attitudes and orientation. It could be one explanation why after a mere fifty years of democracy, judicious and responsible exercise of the freedoms of speech, thought and action still remain a behavioural novelty for the bulk of our people, encouraging licence without responsibility. More ominously, militant ethno-religious dissidence is being actively exploited by hostile external influences to create major internal threats to national security. Tensions are inherent in even the most homogenous societies, but India's socio-religious diversities, economic disparities, and a licentious, irresponsible political culture, have encouraged a surfeit of plagues that are seriously distracting governments from focusing constructively on the urgent priorities of national development. In fact, Indians seem to take a perverse pride in being defiantly ungovernable. It remains to be seen how our existing political, economic and administrative systems will handle these conflicts before they tear the country apart.

We have also to introspect over the political systems we have chosen for ourselves. After fifty years of trial and error, we have transited from democracy with a single political party in power at both Centre and State, to an increasing number of State governments by parties who were in the opposition at the Centre and then to unstable coalitions of disparate political parties in Central governments under pressure from adversarial states. At one level, our long and meandering odyssey can be seen as a model of socio-political evolution in a multi-cultural society. At another, it can also be perceived as a case study of economic development retarded by political instability. Some political parties are suggesting an overhaul of the existing system, with a change to a presidential form of government, which of course is bitterly opposed. However, it may be of relevance to note that notwithstanding their presidential forms of government, governance in both Russia and the USA does not appear to be functioning at all smoothly. In Russia, President Yeltsin is in conflict with the Duma where the opposition is in a majority, and at one time, tanks of the Russian Army were ordered to shell the National Parliament building to force recalcitrant but democratically elected opposition deputies to surrender. In the USA, the acrimonious stand-off between the majority Republicans and Democrat President Clinton has paralyzed coherent governance. In our own country, a cabinet form of parliamentary democracy has not fared much better either and a constant search for elusive consensus amongst disparate political allies has equally paralysed positive governance. The nature of democracy makes it a slow-growing organism, but rapid economic development in a fast-changing international environment cannot afford uncertainty and delay either. We have to devise a constitutional via media that will provide for both stable democracy and rapid development. Does such a solution exist?

The external environment is not encouraging either, and our national security hovers in an uncertain atmosphere. Pakistan, since 1947, and the People's Republic of China, since 1962, have been our traditional external security concerns. Their alliance has confronted India with the classic strategic problem of a two-front military deployment stretching from the Rann of Kutch in the west, via Jammu and Kashmir and the Siachen Glacier in the extreme north of Ladakh, all the way to the Lohit Frontier Division of Arunachal Pradesh in the extreme east.

The Islamic Republic of Pakistan is our closest neighbour, as well as our most consistently hostile adversary. The division of the subcontinent on the basis of religion had been construed by some in Pakistan as a continuation of the historic destiny of Islam on the subcontinent, a march that has to be resumed after an interruption for two centuries by the British presence. This mindset has given us three declared wars with Pakistan, and now a fourth undeclared one that is ongoing at present. Our differences are unlikely to be resolved smoothly, since they really stem not so much from even ostensibly major core issues like Kashmir, but reach further back to a deeper and more complex clash of historical attitudes and emotions, which are much harder to rationalize and reconcile.

In the third of its wars against India, Pakistan lost its colony in the East, which revolted against the domination by the western region, and became the Republic of Bangladesh. The spirit of "badla"—revenge—for this defeat has reinforced Pakistan's traditional hatred of India. Drawing upon its experiences in the CIA-sponsored conflict against the Russian Army, Pakistan has succeeded in exploiting the opportunities created by our own political and administrative blunders and mismanagement in Punjab, Jammu and Kashmir and our Northeast states to launch an Afghanistan-style proxy war targeting these regions. This low intensity conflict which has been ongoing since 1985 is in effect a full-fledged, but undeclared, fourth Indo-Pak War. Pakistan has become a sanctuary for fundamentalist forces like the Taliban, the Harkat-ul-Mujaheddin, the Lashkar-e-Toiba as well as others run by figures like the now well-known Osama bin Laden. These terrorist groups are funded mainly by Saudi Arabian sources, and are motivated to follow obscurantist Wahabi philosophies preaching "jihad" against secular non-Islamic societies. Pakistan controls them through its Inter-Services Intelligence (ISI), and utilizes their combat potential for its own strategic interests, in which India is obviously a priority target. Our major and most immediate threat with mid-and even long-term implications is therefore the emergence of Pakistan as an international epicentre of Wahabi Islamic fundamentalism, which organizes and supports terrorism and insurgency, not only against the USA and her allies, but also against other secular societies and countries like India. Pakistan has assessed India as a soft state, and is determined to continue the confrontation over Kashmir and other issues until India gives in. Barring an abrupt and totally unforeseen change of heart, the state of confrontation is unlikely to stop.

The explosions of Pakistan's Islamic bomb in May 1998 at Chagai Hills have added a new dimension to the issue. Pakistan can now be described as the world's only nuclear-capable Islamic terrorist state. Coercive nuclear blackmail is a major force multiplier for an externally sponsored proxy war, which could be employed very effectively in the current Indo-Pak scenario to pressurize India on withdrawal of troops and cessation of counter-insurgency operations in Kashmir, with every probability of subsequent interference under nuclear duress on other issues as well. India is now facing what is probably a unique situation of an actively ongoing low intensity war against a background of declared nuclear equivalence with Pakistan. Conflict management in a situation of multi-level operational challenges will have serious security implications for India.

Our other neighbour is the People's Republic of China, which attained nuclear capability in 1967, and is one of the original members of the Nuclear Five. It maintains massive conventional forces as well. The nation's soft political leadership in 1962 proved to be less than Churchillian in the hour of crisis and collapsed abjectly at the highest level at this first serious challenge to the nation's security. As always, it was the Indian Army that paid the blood-price for unpreparedness due to the naïve and amateurish approach of our national leaders, who had earlier petulantly rejected professional military advice for defence of the

Himalayan regions. There were no national responses to the Chinese offensive, except a tearful farewell broadcast to Assam by a shell-shocked Prime Minister. The unspoken shadow of that national trauma influences our strategic thinking even today.

We should note that after the Sino-Indian Border War of 1962, there have been no other open military conflicts with China, in spite of the turbulence of a thirty-six year military standoff in the Himalayas, earlier Chinese support to anti-Indian insurgent groups in the North East, build-up of Pakistan as an anti-Indian military surrogate, and sporadic flashpoints at Nathu La in 1967, or Wang Dung-Sumdorong Chu in 1990. Talks to settle the outstanding issues received an impetus after former Prime Minister Rajiv Gandhi's ice-breaking visit to the People's Republic in 1988, and progress has been reasonably responsive since then, but some hiccups were caused by ministerial statements when the present Government assumed office. With China, our differences have been over geographical boundaries, based on conflicting perceptions and interpretations of history. De-escalation is a very desirable strategic goal here, and talks with China on the boundary issues must be followed up in spite of temporary setbacks. As part of its programme of Four Modernizations, China has also embarked on an extensive programme of modernization of its armed forces including major enhancements of nuclear, missile and force projection capabilities. This will widen the military gap even further, but the future prognosis for Sino-Indian relations need not necessarily be pessimistic. Boundary disputes are a common enough phenomenon amongst many neighbouring countries, and our differences are not of such major dimensions that cannot be settled by pragmatic discussions. However, it is also true that peaceful progress on contentious issues is greatly facilitated if the velvet glove of diplomacy is known to be backed up by a substantial mailed fist of military capability. Dialogues and discussions between two large nations cannot be productive, unless carried out as between equals. Military capability still remains a major indicator of national capability, and China's large military and nuclear potential indirectly relegates India to a disadvantaged junior partner in any Sino-Indian negotiations. Strength respects strength, and is a fact of international realpolitik as well as of history. We ignore only at our peril.

Meanwhile, the increasingly intrusive presence of the USA as the sole and dominant economic and military superpower is another factor we have to take note of in our national security equations. No other nation in the world today is capable of militarily or economically challenging the imposition of Pax Americana. The USA, with its camp follower, Britain, is determined to be everyone's friendly neighbourhood policeman, and maintain the primacy of American and Western interests worldwide for which coercive economic, political, and national security interests of nations outside the First World power bloc have become increasingly irrelevant. The United Nations and its Security Council, multilateral funding agencies like the World Bank and the International Monetary Fund, economic regulatory bodies like the World Trade Organization are all heavily dependent on American financial contributions, and are becoming front organizations to put a stamp of international approval on American actions in support of its own interests. The USA has also proclaimed its right to take unilateral action in defence of American interests anywhere in the world, even outside the purview of the United Nations if necessary. Our nuclear programmes, Kashmir, and intellectual property rights, are some of the issues where we must be prepared to ward off adverse pressure from the West. Some statements issued after the recent visit of the US ambassador to Nagaland, may signal the opening of new pressure points in the Northeast as well.

We must understand that all these threats, challenges and pressures to our economy, stability and security will accompany the nation into the twenty-first century also. The millennium will not bring with it any sudden transformations in society, human nature, or the world economic order, and the environment is only likely to grow harsher with the passage of time. Competition between nations is becoming increasingly combative, and the twenty-first century is shaping up to be an era of hard-edged competition and strife for which today's India is singularly ill-prepared. Our narrow sectarian squabbles, petty personalized politics, and lack of statesmanlike, visionary leadership over the past decades has severely retarded our rump to the tryst with destiny that we had visualized at the dawn of Independence on 15 August 1947. Now we may be fated to greet the new millennium as a stunted nation whose full potential is not yet even begun to be realized, even after fifty years of Independence, and will enter the race for a place in the sun in the twenty-first century with many handicaps.

Is it too late for us? Not yet, perhaps, but I do believe it will soon be, unless we take strong affirmative action even at this stage, to redeem our destiny and win back for our present and future generations the promise of prosperity, security and honour in the next century. It is my firm belief that all political and economic systems are equally workable, but the quality of output of any political party when in public office depends on the people they have inducted into the government. The election manifestos of most political parties in India, whether of the Right or of the Left, tend to enunciate almost similar approaches to basic issues of general public concern, including on economic policies with only cosmetic variations, but the choice of language and rhetoric is strongly adversarial, to maintain their respective political appearances. Ultimately, therefore, failure of national governance becomes a failure of human endeavour on a national scale. Our salvation as a nation lies in a return to our roots, to a revival of the human values and principles of our freedom struggle, to Gandhiji's concept of Swadeshi or national self-reliance, and to Netaji Subhas Bose's Itmad, Ittehad, Qurbani, or Confidence, Unity, and Sacrifice—his motto for the Azad Hind Fauj. The basic overarching concept has to be of strong willed national self-reliance, backed by robust self-confidence in our capabilities and achievements, not only in our economic structure, but extended also to the creation of a stable, secular, value-based society, dwelling within secure, strongly-held internal and external boundaries. Unfortunately, Netaji's call to the Indian National Army has been forgotten, while adversarial political relationships and intemperate squabbling between petty unprincipled politicians have coloured even Gandhiji's Swadeshi with pejorative factionalised connotations. The freedom struggle in the present century must become our positive inspiration to launch another and even more crucial effort in the twenty-first century—this time a War of National Renaissance. The struggle for renaissance will have to be in every sense a war for the nation's soul, a Dharma Yuddha, jihad, and a crusade of the Indian nation, as intense as any we have fought on the battlefield in defence of the nation so far. Our country will have to muster all its material and spiritual resources involving every facet of our society and polity, and all our citizens will have to become combatants in the struggle, which will and will have to be vigorously conducted on multiple fronts—economic, spiritual, industrial, social, technological and political—and when necessary, on the ultimate battlefields of armed combat as well.

National renaissance must commence at the top, and seek to refurbish, reconstruct and strengthen our polity, system of governance, and the edifice of national values, which have been severely strained and damaged almost beyond repair in the torments of the last fifty years. The present system has given the country sophisticated political machinery, but no constructive democracy, plenty of expert politicians, but very few genuine statesmen. Policies have become an end in themselves, rather than a means to bring good governance to the people. It is therefore a matter of urgency for this huge nation of almost one billion souls to devise a suitable polity so that national affairs are guided by the distilled essence of the vast and varied human talent available to us, but who somehow cannot find a place in the present system of governance. The only available option seems to be the path towards some form of national government, which will induct the best available talent into the business of governance, nation-wide at the Centre, state-wide in the states, with local extensions of the same principle at every level of government envisaged. But it will be realistic to assume that with all its cancerous manifestations, the existing multi-party system of policies cannot be dislodged or whisked away at least in the short-term perspective. But can these very political parties be reformed or regulated to become the vehicles of change the nation and its polity immediately and desperately require? The concept is known, but the detailed organizational architecture will have to be determined. Implementation of a government of national talent will strike at the roots of all the self-centred vested political interests in the country, and will naturally evoke strong opposition. It is here that we have to regulate, if necessary, compel, political parties to incorporate persons of expertise, talent and, above all, integrity, as their choice of electoral candidates, rather than selecting them on the basis of narrow sectarian or other considerations, which is the norm at present. Our courts of law and statutory bodies like the Election Commission have taken path-breaking steps towards enforcement of good governance and some semblance of election decencies in our political processes. Perhaps these are the agencies, which have to now take further strides to give our great but benighted country the governance we deserve.

Renaissance must also ensure the growth of a prosperous nation, based on strong economic independence and immunization of domestic markets from motivated pressures by developed economies seeking markets for their own goods and services at the expense of indigenous industry. Swadeshi, or national self-reliance in matters economic has been a saviour when tough-mindedly implemented as an instrument of nation-building by other Asian countries like Japan and South Korea. Yet in the politico-economic environments of its own birthplace, Swadeshi has become the centre of intemperate, petty-minded debate by simple-minded, semi-literate politicians, as well as slick, designer-dressed Harvard-oriented economists. After years of acquiescence in the mismanagement of a socialist-oriented economy, the more upmarket section of the bureaucracy too favours uninhibited privatization. The Indian corporate world is split between the new-protectionist votaries of level playing fields, and those supporting the large-scale induction of resource partnerships to bring in foreign capital. As in all such cases, the answer has of necessity to lie somewhere around the median point of all these factors. We have to adopt a combination of free enterprise regulated by strong statutory vigilance, with government guidance and intervention wherever necessary. Totally unregulated laissez faire free enterprise is unsuited to the ethos and ethics in our country. There has to be a place for an efficient de-bureaucratized public sector in essential areas of strategic industries or public infrastructure, which may be either too sensitive for total privatization or essential but commercially unattractive areas where the private sector may not come forward. But our greatest economic asset and strength is the potential market size of the country as an attraction for foreign investment, which must be exploited for both economic as well as strategic reasons. Substantial foreign capital investments and creation of high-value industrial assets, establish binding international commitments, which bring strategic benefits as bargaining counters in negotiations. China has skilfully exploited the economic factor to repeatedly face down the USA when trade and commerce were sought to be conditionally linked with extraneous issues like human rights, devolution of democracy, or freedom of religion in China.

Restoration and enforcement of social stability in the country is paramount during the present period of intense and sometimes violent re-structuring of our society, our polity, and our economic system. Successful nation building depends to a very large degree on a dynamic and interactive equilibrium between the basic triad of Economic Prosperity, Social Stability, and National Security. The best-designed economic programmes will remain stunted and non-performing unless supported by an internal and external growth environment of peace, stability and human motivation. This is being borne out by events in Russia, Indonesia, as well as in other countries. Kashmir and the North-eastern states are examples in our own country, where the unstable security environment has totally halted economic development of the region. Political, social, educational and cultural initiatives are important accompaniments for economic policies, but these may be inadequate in themselves in the face of internal violence and external pressures. Adequate resources and efforts have to be allotted equally for economic development, internal enforcement of governance within the country, as well as defence against external threats, aggression and hostile pressures. The various facets of progress are interdependent and shortfalls in one retard the progress of the others. The country therefore cannot afford to focus on any one aspect alone to the exclusion of all else. Our survival as a competitive nation in the harsh international environment of the next millennium also demands a change in attitudes and approach. We can no longer afford to drift along as a soft effete democracy in a highly challenging international environment that has little time for losers. India has become an example of par excellence of the ultimate soft state, with a permissive "anything-goes" ethos. We have to evolve a functional democracy that also manifests itself as a hard, "zero-tolerance" republic where the rights of the individual are strictly protected, but strong law enforcement also preserves the collective rights of the society and the state. Good governance must be equated with effective governance and in the scheme of things this cannot be achieved by persuasion and consensus alone. It also requires enforcement of laws for the collective-well-being of the country and the government will always require a credible assertive capability to ensure this by way of viable defence forces and effective policing organizations.

The present generations appear to be witnessing an inexplicable and all-pervasive death-wish that seems to have gripped every aspect of constructive national endeavour. In fact these unsettled conditions may well be normal during a time of social change, which we, purely by historical coincidence, are probably involuntary witness to. We may be living through an era of a gathering convulsion, which in its scope, content and ultimate intensity may well be judged in retrospect to have been on par with the French, Russian, or the cultural revolutions. It is under these conditions of almost endemic internal turmoil that our journey into the twenty-first century will take place.

National power is the currency that will determine our status and standing in the world community. Ultimately, it will be our national power alone that will finally determine whether we remain what we are today—a nation of great potential, but retarded development, or do finally succeed in graduating to the status of a major power.

And finally, a voice from the past: "India, the ancient Mother, is indeed striving to be reborn, striving with agony and tears, but she strives in vain. What ails her, she who is after all so vast, and might be so strong? There is surely some enormous defect, something vital is wanting in us, nor is it difficult to lay our finger on the spot. We have all things else, but are empty of strength, void of energy. We have abandoned Shakti, and are therefore abandoned by Shakti. Many of us are saying nowadays that it is impossible, that India is decayed, bloodless and lifeless, too weak ever to recover; that our race is doomed to extinction. It is a foolish and idle saying. No man or nation needs to be weak unless he chooses, no man or nation need perish unless he deliberately chooses extinction. For what is a nation? What is our mother country? It is not a piece of earth, nor a figure of speech nor a fiction of the mind. It is a mighty Shakti, composed of the Shaktis of all the millions of units that make up the nation—The Shakti we call India, Bhawani, Bharati".

Sri Aurobindo, one of India's greatest sons, wrote this cry from the heart in 1904 in his revolutionary proclamation, "Bhawani Mandir." As the new millennium approaches, the nation waits at the same crossroads today.

Thank you.

Jai Hind

14

Safeguarding Unity and Integration of the Indian Nation

Nani A. Palkhivala,
Indian Jurist and Liberal Economist

The unity of India is vital for the survival of freedom in our country, and that is why it has been specifically referred to in the preamble of our Constitution. The integration of our various communities is indispensable to our unity. The nagging question, which will not go away, is—Is India a collection of communities or is it a nation? In other words, is India a state without a nation?

The greatest achievement of Indian democracy has been that it has survived unfractured for more than forty-five years. Nine hundred and eighty million people—more than the combined population of Africa and South America—live together as one political entity under conditions of freedom. Never before in history, and nowhere else in the world today, has one-sixth of the human race existed as a single free nation.

The achievement is all the more creditable since no other democracy has had such diversity in unity and presents such a mosaic of humanity. All the well-known religions of the world flourish in India. We have sixteen major languages, written in different alphabets, and derived from different roots; and for good measure, our people—whom you can never call taciturn—express themselves in two hundred and fifty dialects. English, which is not included in the major languages listed in the constitution, yet continues to be the only link language for the whole country.

In 1950, we started as a republic with three inestimable advantages.

First, we had 5000 years of civilization behind us—a civilization that had reached "the summit of human thought" in the words of Ralph Waldo Emerson. We had inherited great skills and many—splendoured intelligence, since the genes had evolved over five luminous millennia. We had a superb entrepreneurial spirit, honed over a century of obstacles. A few years ago a World Bank report on India mentioned two very favorable factors—an unlimited reservoir of skilled labour, and abundance of capital available for investment in new projects. The trader's instinct is innate in Indian genes. An Indian can buy from a Jew and sell to a Scot, and yet make a profit!

Secondly, whereas before 1858 India was never a united political entity, in that year the accident of British rule welded us into one country, one nation; and when independence came, we had been in unified nationality for almost a century under one head of state.

You have only to contrast the disadvantages under which a nation would have to begin its life as a republic, when advantages of the type, which accrued to India from British rule, do not exist. Take the thirteen colonies in America which won their independence in 1783. Those thirteen colonies were bound together merely by loose articles of confederation. They had no unified nationality, no head of state, no central government, no central judiciary, no common taxation, and no national currency. On all those points, the Raj supplied India with the benefits, which the United States of America lacked. India could not, and would not, have reached its present level without the fortuity of British Raj.

Thirdly, our Founding Fathers after three long years of laborious and painful toil, gave us a Constitution, which a former Chief Justice of India rightly described as "sublime". It was the longest constitution in the world till, a few years ago, Yugoslavia had the impertinence to adopt a longer constitution!

The substance of the Universal Declaration of Human Rights adopted by the United Nations on 10th December 1948 is embodied as Fundamental Rights in our Constitution. The right to equality before the law is guaranteed to citizens and non-citizens alike. In one respect our constitutional law is more secular than that of the United Kingdom—religion is no bar the holding of any public office whatsoever in the State. In other respect, our constitution may claim to be more progressive than that of the USA—equality of the sexes is a guaranteed right in India, whereas the recent attempt to incorporate a similar right in the US Constitution has so far been unsuccessful.

The right to carry on any occupation, trade or business is, again, a guaranteed right. The concept of doctrinaire "socialism" did not figure anywhere in the Constitution as originally enacted. On the contrary, the Constitution provided in the Directive Principles of State Policy that the State shall endeavor to secure that "the ownership and control of the material resources of the community are so disturbed as best to subserve the common good" and that "the operation of the economic system does not result in the concentration of wealth and means of production to the common detriment." These words rule out State ownership—the Monolithic State—which is the hallmark of communism, euphemistically called socialism.

India is the only country in the world where, in the States, which are governed by the Communist Party, human rights are fully respected—and that is only because the Bill of Rights is firmly ingrained in our national Constitution.

We can proudly say that our Constitution, which enjoins the unity and integrity of India, gave us a flying start; and equipped us adequately to meet the challenges of the future. Unfortunately, over the years we dissipated every advantage we started with, like a compulsive gambler bent upon squandering an invaluable legacy. I am afraid India today is only a caricature of the noble democracy which Jawaharlal Nehru strove to bring to life and freedom in 1947, and which our constitution envisaged in 1950.

Never before in our republic's history has violence marked our national life on a scale so widespread as at present. We have enough religion to hate one another but not enough to love one another.

Unfortunately, religious fanaticism has become a global phenomenon and prompts more than twenty per cent of international terrorist incidents.

At a colloquium held last month in Paris, Paul Wilkinson, an authority on terrorism, said, "If I had been giving this talk in the 1960's there would have not been a single major terrorist organization at that time that would have had a religious motivation.... Today religious fanatics see unbelievers as expendable and somehow lacking in the status of full humanity." India has more than its fair share of religious fanaticism.

One may apply to India the words used by the late Benigno Aquino about the Philippines—"Here is a land in which a few are spectacularly rich while the masses remain abjectly poor...where freedom and its blessings are reality for minority and an illusion for the many...a land consecrated to democracy but...a land of privilege and rank...a republic dedicated to equality but mired in an archaic system of caste."

The greatest problem of India is that its finest men—men of caliber and vision, knowledge and character—are not in politics and stand little chance of getting elected having regard to the murky atmosphere of our political life. Caste is the football in the political game which our men in public life play.

Unfortunately, divisiveness has become the Indian disease. Truly, divisiveness is the Aids of India—a disease which is spreading fast and wide, preys on the public mind and is without a cure in sight. Communal hatred, linguistic fanaticism and regional loyalty are gnawing at the vitals of the unity and integrity of the country. To the growing army of terrorists and professional hooligans, caste or clan, creed or tongue, is a sufficient ground to kill their fellow citizens.

The most carrying need of India today is to undergo catharsis, a course of emotional cleansing. We must not allow the moral bedrock of our society to turn to lava.

National integration is born in the hearts if the citizens. When it dies there, no army, no government, no constitution, can save it. States of mind precede states. Inter-faith harmony and consciousness of the essential unity of all religions is the very heart of our national integration. The soul of India aspires to integration and assimilation. Down the ages, Indian culture—a tremendous force of power and beauty has been, made richer and deeper as a result of absorbing what is best in outside influences and integrating those various influences to grace and enrich its own identity.

In the history of India which goes back five thousand years, the British connection has only been a short episode. It was a brief interlude lasting less than a century from the Proclamation by Queen Victoria in 1858 to the grant of independence in 1947; less than two centuries if we start with the first significant act of British dominion, the Battle of Plassey in 1757; and less than four centuries if we count from the incorporation of the East India Company in 1600.

I hope we shall always have enough large—heartedness to admit that the largesse of the English language enriched Indian culture. It was the cement, which bound and continues to bind, our country together; and it enabled us to deal with the rest of the world from a vantage point. As I said before, there are sixteen major Indian languages listed in the Constitution, and each of them is used by tens of millions. Those who are following the developments in Canada which has only two languages, English and French, can imagine the multiplication of the problems where sixteen state languages are spoken by different groups who are not unfamiliar with linguistic fanaticism. Even today, the south will not accept any communication from the north in Hindi, which is the language of the north, but is willing to accept all communications in English. The authentic text of our constitution is in English; the laws are passed by our Parliament in English, justice is administered invariably by the Supreme Court in English and usually by the eighteen High Courts in English. It is interesting to note that four of the first thirteen awards of the Booker Prize were either to Indians or for books about India. *The Times* editorially noted on February 11, 1992:

> *"...Indian English is in some ways more correct than British English, because it is taught from old-fashioned textbooks by teachers for whom it is not their first language. There may well be fewer unconscious solecisms and barbarisms in Indian English than in British. Indians are less casual with the shared language."*

The civil and criminal laws, apart from personal laws applicable to particular communities, are based upon English jurisprudence. The main instrument of criminal justice—the Indian Penal Code—was drafted by Lord Macaulay when he functioned as the Law Minister of India from 1834 to 1838. It is a tribute to his superb draftsmanship that the Indian Penal Code is one of the least amended statutes of India.

Broadly speaking, the administrative structure in India is still as the British left it. The Indian Civil Service (ICS) started by the British was, beyond question, one of the finest civil services the world has ever known. Sardar Vallabhbhai Patel had the good sense to recognize this, and when he introduced the Indian Administrative Services (IAS) it was based on the model of the ICS. At the same time it must be confessed that while the top ICS officers were outstanding, the bureaucratic structure, which the British created, left much to be desired.

Not the least of the gifts that the British left behind was the institution of the armed forces imbued with the tradition of being totally apolitical. Today when we see corruption and degradation all round in India, the one institution of which we can be justly proud is that of the Armed forces. In point of discipline and dedication, efficiency and competence, it is equal of its counterpart anywhere in the world.

Finally, paradoxical as it may seem, if India is a free republic today, that is also the consequence of British rule. Indians fought, and fought valiantly, to get rid of foreign domination. But it is probable that up to now India would not have shaken off the domination of Indian rulers but for the notions of freedom imbibed from the days of British rule. Macaulay foresaw this development. He said, "By good government we may educate our subjects [so] that they may in some future age demand European institutions. Whenever such a day comes, it will be the proudest day in English history."

Let me cast a glance at what the future portends for India.

A nation's worth is not measured merely by its gross national product, any more than an individual's worth is measured by his bank account. Ambassador John Kenneth Galbraith remarked that while he had seen poverty in many countries of the world, he found one unusual attribute among poor of India.—"There is richness in their poverty". They do not count their wealth in money alone.

The heart of the nation is sound and the human raw material is excellent. To a western mind, the Indian's inner strength and capacity for patience and endurance are almost unbelievable.

Hundreds of millions, who have no standard of living, still have a standard of life. The nation is able to take in its stride situations which would cause a revolution in other countries. The ancient civilization has survived and will survive when the raucous and fractious voices of today are lost in the silence of the centuries.

Nature has been kind to India in one respect. It has endowed the country with the gift of producing great leaders in the darkest hour—leaders with the gift of grace who can arouse the trusting millions to great heights. Look at the galaxy of character and caliber India produced at the time of struggle for independence in the thirties and the forties.

When the hour struck, the man was found—Mahatma Gandhi—the greatest of our integrators. He lit the imagination of the entire nation. He created men out of dust. He taught the unforgettable lesson that cynicism corrupts and absolute cynicism absolutely. He made us realize the profound truth that the single minded pursuit of money impoverishes the mind, shrivels the imagination, and desiccates the heart.

There is a basic lesson of Indian history. Our people have always taken their moral standards from their rulers: the people have risen to great heights when they have basked in the glow of noble kings of leaders. The present generation is waiting for a leader who will make it relearn the moral values, and who will inculcate in the people, as Gandhi did, a sense of the responsibilities which fall on every citizen of a free society.

One last thought and I shall have done. Today, the unity and integrity of India seems to be at stake. But "even this shall pass away". Indian society will, in course of time, acquire the requisite political culture—the attitudes had habits of tolerance, mutual respect and goodwill, which alone can make democracy workable.

The day will come when the 25 states of India will realize that in a profound sense they are culturally akin, ethnically identical, linguistically knit and historically related. The greatest task before India today is to acquire a keener sense of national identity, to gain the wisdom to cherish its priceless heritage, and to create a cohesive society with the cement of Indian culture. We shall then celebrate the 15th day of August not as the Day of Independence but as the Day of Interdependence—the dependence of the States upon one another, the dependence of our numerous communities upon one another, the dependence of the many castes and clans upon one another—in the sure knowledge that we are one nation.

Safeguarding the unity and integrity of the Indian nation is essential to the very survival of our freedom. This is the main theme of the thoughtful and thought-provoking book, PREPARE OR PERISH, published in 1991 by General Krishna Rao, the former Chairman of the Chiefs of Staff, and the present Governor of Jammu and Kashmir. General Krishna Rao quotes the lines of Rudyard Kipling, which, I hope, will always remain engraved on the mind of every Indian:

Nations have passed away and left no traces,
And History gives the naked cause of it.
One single, simple reason in all cases;
They fell because their people were not fit.

15

Role of Universities towards the Armed Forces

General Bipin Chandra Joshi,
PVSM, AVSM, ADC,
Chief of the Army Staff

I am very charged with emotion. I hope being a soldier of close to 44 years of training, it will be a controlled display of emotional outburst. I consider myself twice blessed because as I occupy this rostrum with humility I am reflecting over my academic record, when in 1950, having done my 10 + 2, I became a candidate for commissioning into noble profession of Arms. And then, without having seen the inside of the highest temple of learning, in 1990, I was awarded an M.Sc. degree from the Madras University, without any questions asked if I had done my graduation and as if that was not enough and to prove that it was not a fluke, the Kumaon University this year decided to award the Doctor of Science degree to me. So, with such an uneducated background, to be in the company of Gurus who represent the who's who of the highest learning in our country it requires humility to absorb such a great honour. And I hope I will bear up to this.

Why I consider myself twice blessed is that the first portal of high learning that I had the privilege of entry was in Pune, when Prof. Gupte asked me to deliver the convocation address. Till then, this kind of privilege was not due to me because of my poor academic background. That it happens to be in Maharashtra, that it happens to be in Pune, which has got one of the finest traditions of higher learning in our country and without sounding parochial, I almost feel that I am in the intellectual capital of our country. That is why I consider myself, twice blessed. So, I promise you that in the following few minutes I will talk to you and not at you when I share some of my concerns and aspirations about the involvement of the citizenry and the academia of our great country in affairs, military, in national security and in national development. In a manner of speaking, I am making a humble attempt to arouse to activate your military *Kundalini,* and I hope. I am successful at the end of it. I say so this today with a sense of great urgency on four counts.

Firstly, in my study of the Indian and international scene, I have already come across 10 manifestations that have convinced me and which have emboldened me to declare my assessment that the next century, which is a mere six years away, is going to be India's century. This is not building castles in the air. It has the strength of whatever its worth of the considered assessment of a soldier, who must not be given to over statement. The question I think, which is begging the answer is: Is it going to happen because of us or in spite of us? That is the urgency that I am keen that it happens because of us.

The second, the Indian Army today is deficient of Officer Strength, of a mind-boggling figure of 12,500, which makes me 30 per cent short of my authorized strength. And I regretfully want to admit that the country is not giving me the best. What I have got, what I have managed to bring into shape is good enough. But, I am afraid the country is not giving the military the best, which it has to offer. I want to raise the question, "Does this great country want to have first class defence with second-rate input or second-rate material?". So, there is urgency. I must appeal to you to bear these concerns with you.

The third is that the military today sends out of uniform, because of its narrow pyramid, something like 70,000 to 80,000 personnel whose ages range between 35 and 56, which is patriotic, fiercely patriotic, disciplined and developed. And this great country of ours has not been able to innovate an institution that can harness this talent for the country's development and for the country's future. So, I thought I should appeal to those who, like me, are also developers of human resources, i.e., the august body of Vice-Chancellors and the University Grants Commission. There is no point having a Ministry of Human Resource Development on one side and discarding developed, discipline and patriotic human resources at the same time. You are losing money twice over.

And the fourth one, the last one but not the least, we are as indeed all countries in the world are, in the throes of a resource crunch because we need to do so much for our country and for our citizenry and the money is limited. So, in terms of defence, this resource crunch means that the Indian genius must find an answer to have optimum defence at an affordable cost. This will require the best brains of the country to study the subject and come up with innovative answers. So, I believe ladies and gentlemen, we have already let the situation assume urgency by not dealing with it when it was necessary. We must not permit a situation where this urgency degenerates into criticality. Because, then the price may be unaffordable.

What, in my humble view, is the role of the universities in this endeavour is what I have tried to focus attention on. In a recent book which has been published by an American, it says that "Indian Vedas recognized 24 *Vidyas* and it is enshrined there that matters military, strategy and indeed military technology as well as the military art and science are featured among these 24 *Vidyas*". It needs no reiteration that *Kautilya,* the greatest Indian enunciator of a security doctrine and the only enunciator of a security doctrine-cum-practitioner, who in the 4th century BC conceived a strategy and implemented it to create the *Mauryan Empire,* did his homework in the portals of Takshashila University. We will at our peril lose sight of this fact. In the USA, the finest papers on matters military are thrown up by Stanford University, Columbia University and the like, including the academia, which forms part of the Rand Corporation of the Ford Foundation.

Our *Shastras* have taught six *Shakthis.*

The first is the *Mantra,* which is *Mantra and Mantrana.* That makes two of these. Then you have the *Jan Shakthi* and then the *Utsah* and the last but the most important is the *Prabhu Shakthi,* which is the combination of *Kosh,* i.e., *Economics* and *Dand,* which is the military. Does it need reiteration on my part to remind the academia and ask whether we are paying enough attention to the *Sixth Shakthi,* not necessarily in the order of preferences, i.e., *Dand*? Should it not be the business of the academia to assess the endeavour to make this country powerful by not neglecting the study of the *Sixth Shakthi*, which is part of *Prabhu Shakthi*.

I have come across certain parameters in our country's history, which are clear indicators of whether this country is on the right or the wrong path and I venture to share my analysis with you. And these are four parameters of India's strength.

Firstly, it is the quality of *Dharmacharis*. It is because of this that in ancient India the preceptor or the *Purohit* of the *Yuvaraj* and the *Senapathi* were given the second place in the order of precedence, after the King himself. And I believe that the preceptors of this country have an abode in the portals of these universities. And you are the ones who are creating the *Dharmacharis* of tomorrow.

The second one is the state of the *Guru-Shishya Parampara*. Whenever this *Parampara* has been in on an even keel, India has prospered. Whenever, for whatever reason, this *Parampara* has been permitted to decline or degenerate, it has identified itself or manifested itself in the degeneration of the nation itself. So, that is your role that is your stake.

The third one is the relationship between politics and the *academia*. I believe a good academia like a good military must be apolitical. But this does not mean that either the military or the academia or both should be political ignoramuses. What it means is they shall not play politics, particularly if it tends to be dirty and murky...... There will have to be adventure in ideas or *Swaraj* in ideas and the right place to indulge in this activity is the sanctimonious portals of our temples of higher learning.

So, if these were the parameters and the indicators, the responsibility, the partnership, the role and the stake of the academia and the military is absolutely clear. Having analyzed and delved on the necessity, let me identify from my long list of subjects that we could study, a few that need to be studied immediately.

The first is what I call the Colonel Blimp image of the military officers. Of the seven images that are doing the rounds in this country, this is easily the most devastating and is signified in our pictures, when you have a Colonel Sahib with the golf cap and plus fours and a gun in hand. And whenever any family or any segment of society has any problems, they run up to the Colonel Sahib and his immediate answer to them is that he shoots first and asks questions later. And when he is nervous, he puffs at his pipe.

A great or at least regarded as a great politician of France, Clemenceau, said, "*War is too serious a business to be left to the Generals*". The military leadership of the time retorted that "*war is too serious a business to be left to the politicians.*" The time has come when the four important channels of inter-state contact, i.e., the political, the diplomatic, the economic and the military-to-military-contact and all the politicians, the academics, the economists, the diplomats and the soldiers should join the national endeavour to make the country great.

I just would like to pose a question. If in 1962, there were a military-to-military contact with our adversary of the time, would the history of the 1962 conflict have been different? This question needs to be studied. We have just about started coming out of the psychological trauma of that minor aberration that took place at that point of time. Now, I think, we have to study what could have happened if we had a contact at this level.

Defence and development is often projected by those who still get their inspiration from Whitehall or who are carrying in brown colour the white man's burden in our country. And it is projected as a conflict between development and defence because in the Keynesian concept of economics, defence is a non-plan and non-development expenditure. But we are forgetting that in a third world country like India, which some have called a poor developed country, how many budgets have been paid for by the security that the military has provided, the national morale that the military has upheld, the far-flung areas of our country that we have opened and indeed in the field of adventure, in sports and ecology the contribution that has been made by the Armed Forces. I like to suggest that at least 20 times the money has been already paid back. If the project study of a factory can include the walls that surround the factory and its watch-and–ward staff, I don't see why a high-value target of something like Rs. 10,000 crore in the form of Bombay High should not pay for its defence through a few naval ships. These are thoughts that I think you with the *Swaraj* in ideas and adventure in ideas should articulate in the portals of our temples of learning. We could talk about human rights; it must not be left only to the Chief of the Indian Army to issue his *Ten Commandments*. I believe it is the concern of the entire country.

Have we really studied our present and prospective enemies? Even *Sage Kautilya* when he made the *Saptang* theory of State, I believe and I say it with great reverence and great humility and not with criticism, left out the eighth ingredient, i.e., the knowledge of the enemy. Should we not be studying Pakistan and China in an institutionalized manner? And throwing up formulations, which will excite the entire country? I could go on and on.

But having said all this, I think I should now put across a small blueprint or a five-fold mantra of my aspirations for your consideration. I believe we must have more seats of higher learning for our defence officers in selected subjects, which can be studied by them in the universities without having too many procedural impediments. One extension of this, perhaps, because of my personal experience in the Pune University, is that it will make me and the Indian Army and the Indian Military feel very happy if the nodal agency for this were the Pune University because in this town we have about 25 defence establishments of various disciplines and we can use Pune University's contribution on this historic occasion. I think I can fix them and request them to be termed as a nodal agency to coordinate this on an all-India basis.

The second point is, perhaps, arranging some facilities for sabbaticals for senior officers of the Indian Army of periods extending from 3 to 24 months where, I will spare officers of the rank of Brigadier and above and you will give them place and the time to take leave of their day-to-day worries and indulge in this adventure in ideas.

The third one is that we have established one chair, but I am told the number of Vice-Chancellors present here itself is three. So, we want to add perhaps a couple of zeros not on the left-hand side of this one but on the right hand side. And I would urge this audience and this august body to deliberate over it and to bring joy to the country by studying the country's problems in an institutionalized manner in an atmosphere that is conducive.

Perhaps the fourth suggestion I could venture now is about joint subcontracting of research projects to institutions other than the tertiary level of education. Now, what would the army do in return? Because there has to be a quid pro quo in today's economic world. And the quid pro quo on the part of Army is that while we are attempting to do our job even at the risk of the supreme sacrifice, the military will ensure that *India is not permitted to die*. That is a promise of blood, that is a promise of sacrifice, for all the goodies that the academic fraternity will shower on the soldiers of India.

Ladies and gentlemen, my final observation of all my study of history and what little I have studied has told me ***"No country really has prospered which has ignored its soldier"***. In India, you created *Dharma* by creating a clan, not by birth but by vocation. And you give it a place. That is your heritage that is your tradition, that is your stake and your role is clear.

With this, I come to an end. I hope my attempts to arouse or to activate your *Kundalini* have been a pleasurable experience for you.

I wish and I pray that it enters the *Sahasrara* at the earliest.

Thank you!

Index

*